Mind the Gap

Mind the Gap

How the Jewish Writings between the Old and New
Testament Help Us Understand Jesus

Matthias Henze

Fortress Press
Minneapolis

MIND THE GAP
How the Jewish Writings between the Old and New Testament Help Us
Understand Jesus

Cover image: Section from the Psalms Scrolls, Qumran cave 11, ca.
30-50 CE (parchment) / The Israel Museum, Jerusalem, Israel /
Bridgeman Images
Cover design: Tory Herman

Print ISBN: 978-1-5064-0642-8
eBook ISBN: 978-1-5064-0643-5

The paper used in this publication meets the minimum requirements of
American National Standard for Information Sciences — Permanence of
Paper for Printed Library Materials, ANSI Z329.48-1984.

Manufactured in the U.S.A.

Contents

Introduction

A Visitor from Israel

As a teenager growing up in Hanover in northern Germany, I developed an interest in early Christianity and began to read the Bible. One day, as I was browsing in a local bookstore, I saw an announcement that Schalom Ben-Chorin was coming to town to give a public lecture on Jesus. Schalom Ben-Chorin was a Jewish journalist and scholar living in Jerusalem who frequently returned to his native Germany to give talks and teach classes. Over the years, Ben-Chorin became instrumental in initiating the German-Jewish dialogue after the Holocaust. According to the announcement, his talk was titled "Brother Jesus: The Nazarene through Jewish Eyes." (Some years later, Ben-Chorin would publish a book with the same title.) Since I had never heard a presentation by a Jewish scholar, let alone one on Jesus, I became very excited and realized that this would be a special event I had to attend.

The auditorium was packed that evening, and the audience was clearly mesmerized. I don't remember many of the details of the talk, but I do remember that the evening made a lasting impression on me. Schalom Ben-Chorin was soft-spoken and mild mannered, and obviously deeply learned. The Holocaust was still in living memory, only forty years prior. The scars of the war were everywhere. Here was a Jewish scholar who had come all the way from Israel and who stretched out his hand as a demonstrative gesture of reconciliation. Ben-Chorin had come to study with us. There was not a trace of reproach or accusation in his presentation, only the desire to move on, to study together, and to read the New Testament from a Jewish perspective. I had never seen anything quite like this, and, judging by the reaction from the audience, I was not alone.

But it wasn't just the particular situation of learning from a Jewish scholar in post-war Germany that moved me. As I listened to Schalom Ben-Chorin, it occurred to me how little I knew about the world of Jesus, in spite of having studied the New Testament. Jesus was fully immersed in the Jewish world of his time, but I did not recognize or understand much of that world. It seemed foreign to me, remote. I did not recognize the Judaism of Jesus because all I knew was the Old Testament. But the religion of the Old Testament is not the Judaism of Jesus. While in the New Testament, Jesus studies and teaches in the synagogues, there are no synagogues in the Old Testament. While in the New Testament, Jesus's disciples call him rabbi, there are no rabbis in the Old Testament. While in the New Testament, Jesus is often involved in conversations with the Pharisees, there are no Pharisees in the Old Testament. While in the New Testament, Jesus expels demons and unclean spirits, there are no demons in the Old Testament. The list goes on. These are not incidental matters in the life of Jesus. They all stem from the Jewish world to which Jesus belonged, a world about which I knew so little apart from what I had read in the New Testament. I felt that I was rather ill-equipped to be an informed reader of the Bible, whereas for Schalom Ben-Chorin there was nothing strange about this. Clearly, he did not need to be told what a synagogue was, or a rabbi, or who the Pharisees were. To the contrary, he was intimately familiar with the world of his "brother Jesus."

There is something unsettling about coming to realize that the person who stands at the center of the Christian faith, Jesus of Nazareth, the son of Joseph and Mary, was not a Christian but a Jew. For me, it did not help much to recognize how little I knew of Jesus's own religious background. If I didn't understand ancient Judaism very well, how could I understand Jesus? It was much more comfortable to think of Jesus as one of us, somebody who was exactly like we are today, sharing the same theology, the same political points of view, and certainly the same religion. As I once heard it put, God created humankind in God's image (an allusion to the creation of humans in Genesis 1:26–27), and we are quick to return the favor. We like to think of God and of Jesus as if they are just like us. In this reading, there is nothing strange or surprising about the Bible, because we have turned the Bible into a mirror in which all we can see is ourselves. But we cannot see what is actually there: synagogues, rabbis, the Sabbath, Pharisees, demons, and the resurrection—in short, the world of Jesus.

For the longest time, I was under the impression that this is the reason why the Christian Bible has two parts, the Old Testament and the New Testament. I simply assumed that the Old Testament was the Jewish part of the Christian Bible and the New Testament was the Christian part. The purpose of the Old Testament was to explain Judaism to Christians. Whenever we read in the New Testament of Jesus's Judaism, we could simply turn to the Old Testament, and there, somewhere, we would find an explanation for the Jewish world of Jesus. The only problem was that I never seemed to be able to find the relevant passages in the Old Testament. What I found didn't really explain what I was looking for. Surely, I thought, the reason was my insufficient knowledge of the Bible: I was simply looking in the wrong places. Only later did I realize that the mistake was not mine. I was looking for passages about synagogues and rabbis and Pharisees that simply don't exist. The Old Testament cannot explain the Jewish world of Jesus.

The Jewish World of Jesus

Jesus was deeply immersed in the Jewish world of his time. Most Christian readers of the New Testament today cannot understand that world, because what is described in the Old Testament is not the Judaism of Jesus. The Old Testament cannot explain the religious beliefs and practices of Jesus's Judaism because the books of the Old Testament were written hundreds of years before the time of Jesus. The Old Testament remained the foundational sacred text for Jesus and his followers, to be sure, but it was written in a different era. By the time of Jesus, Judaism had evolved in many significant ways. Jews had to respond to a constantly changing political landscape, and they continued to be exposed to various, ever-changing foreign influences. Old ideas had progressed, new ideas had been introduced, other religious movements and Jewish sects had formed, different kinds of religious institutions had been set up, new literary expressions that we do not find in the Old Testament flourished, and many new books had been written. The Jewish world of Jesus was no longer the religious world of the Old Testament, it was the Judaism of first-century Israel.

In order to understand Jesus and his message, we have to have a basic understanding of first-century Judaism. To gain that understanding, reading the Old Testament alone is not enough. Jesus did not emerge from the Old Testament, he emerged from the Judaism of his time. If the Old Testament cannot supply the information we need to understand the Jewish world of the New Testament, what can?

The Bible does not contain all the literature that has come down to us from ancient Israel. In fact, the books of the Old Testament only represent a portion of the vast library of ancient Jewish texts that were in circulation at the time of Jesus. There are many ancient Jewish books outside the Bible that were copied and read in antiquity, and some of them were rather popular in early Christian circles. Fortunately, many of these books have survived and are available to us today. They are not as well-known, because they are not part of our Bibles. The fact that these forgotten books of ancient Israel are not well-known today does not mean that they were equally unpopular in antiquity. Some of these texts, books like 1 Enoch or Jubilees, were considered inspired and authoritative by some ancient groups, just like the books of the Bible. In recent decades, interest in these long-forgotten, ancient Jewish books

4

has increased significantly. There is now a growing awareness, both among scholars and general readers, of the importance of these Jewish texts for the study of ancient Judaism and the beginnings of Christianity. The discovery of the Dead Sea Scrolls in the 1940s and 1950s was a real game-changer in this regard. These ancient Jewish manuscripts have generated enormous energy and a renewed interest in ancient Judaism by opening a window into the fascinating and complex world of pre-Christian Judaism. The aim of this book is to introduce some of these lesser-known books, including some of the Dead Sea Scrolls, and to explain, using specific case studies from the New Testament, how they can shed light on Jesus, his life and message, and in particular the world from which he emerged.

About This Book

This book has two main parts. Part one, "Mind the Gap! Reading between the Old and the New Testament," provides a brief introduction to the history and literature of ancient Israel. Chapter 1 begins with a historical timeline that divides the history of ancient Israel into its major periods. Familiarity with the most important periods and dates of ancient Israel will be useful to gain a better sense of when the books of the Bible were written. The timeline also helps visualize that there is a significant chronological gap of several hundred years between the Old and the New Testament. Chapter 2 introduces some of the books that were written during the gap years between the two Testaments. These are the forgotten books of Jewish antiquity that provide invaluable information about the Jewish world of the New Testament and that we cannot afford to ignore—hence the title, *Mind the Gap*.

Part two of the book, "The Jewish Jesus," contains five chapters. Each of the first four chapters is devoted to a particular case study that demonstrates how ancient Jewish books outside the Bible can help us understand Jesus. Chapter 3 discusses the messianic expectations in Judaism at the turn of the Common Era. The evangelists were keenly aware of these expectations, alluded to them, and used them in their descriptions of Jesus in order to argue that Jesus, the son of Mary and Joseph, was, in fact, the Messiah for whom Israel was waiting. Chapter 4 is devoted to the world of demons and unclean spirits. The existence of these spiritual beings is simply taken for granted in the New Testament and is never explained anywhere in the Bible. However, the Jewish texts outside the Bible provide a great deal of information about the origin of demons and unclean spirits and help us understand why Jesus's acts of exorcism were regarded as so significant. Chapter 5 takes up the classic topic of Jesus and the law of Moses. Against the common belief that Jesus, and Paul after him, dispensed with the law, a careful reading of the pertinent texts in the Gospel of Matthew and Paul's letter to the Romans demonstrates that both Jesus and Paul upheld the centrality of the law and redefined its significance. Chapter 6 addresses the belief in the resurrection of the dead and in life with the angels. That belief was already widespread in Judaism prior to the time of Jesus. The extra-biblical texts demonstrate how it evolved after the Old Testament.

The second part of the book ends with an Epilogue that explains what exactly is at stake when we take seriously that Jesus was a practicing Jew.

Reading the New Testament in the Twenty-First Century

Listening to Schalom Ben-Chorin in that lecture hall in Hanover made me keenly aware of the fact that all biblical interpretation happens at a particular moment in time. That moment is of great significance for how we read the Bible, and it determines to no small degree what it is we are looking for in the biblical text. The followers of Jesus in first-century Israel read their Scriptures differently than we do today. Ancient biblical interpretation requires historical contextualizing, just as modern biblical interpretation is situated in its own particular context. This book, too, occupies a particular place in the academic study of ancient Israel. In the last half century, some very significant changes have occurred in how scholars approach and view the Jewish world of the New Testament. This new approach to the New Testament is very much reflected in the way in which the ancient Jewish books—inside and outside the Old Testament—will be treated in this book.

For many Christian scholars of the late nineteenth century, ancient Jewish literature pointed directly to Jesus. With the appearance of Jesus and his followers, Judaism had lost its relevance and, in a deeper theological sense, its legitimacy. According to some of these Christian scholars, Judaism had become irrelevant, which explains why so many of them have long had a bias against the study of the Judaism of the time of Jesus. Why study a deteriorated form of the Jewish religion? Others went even further. To them, Israel was no longer God's chosen people; it had been replaced by the church. But a reading of the ancient Jewish texts that privileges the New Testament and that is focused exclusively on Jesus overlooks the simple fact that Judaism did not cease to exist with Jesus. Judaism did not die on the cross. It has continued to exist beyond the first century, and it has hardly become irrelevant. To overlook this fact amounts to bad history, and bad history begets bad theology. It is therefore critically important, particularly for the Christian reader of the ancient Jewish texts that form the core of this book, to be mindful that the modern interpretation of ancient Jewish literature cannot be reduced to the question of what these texts have to say about the New Testament. The Jewish texts should be read first and foremost in their own right. Only then should we read them side by side with the New Testament. Put bluntly, rather than reducing ancient Jewish writings to background literature to the New Testament, we should understand the New Testament as part of the much larger world of ancient Judaism.

Vocabulary and Methodology

I should briefly explain some of the terms I will be using throughout this book. (In addition, I have provided a glossary at the end of this book that explains some of the more technical terms that are used in biblical scholarship; the glossary also covers many personal names and book titles.) The question of who is a Jew and what exactly marks the beginning of Judaism continues to be a contentious and much debated issue. It is one of the basic theses of this book that the religion we find in the Old Testament is not the same as the religion of those who lived, and continue to live, as Jews in postbiblical times. As I have heard it put, "The religion *in* the Old Testament is not the same as the religion *of* the Old Testament." In other words, the religion we find described in the Old Testament is very different from the religion of those postbiblical communities, both Jewish and Christian, who follow and live by the Bible as Scripture. Of course, the same could be said about Christianity: the religion of the Christians who live in postbiblical times, including Christianity today, is hardly the same as the religion we find described in the New Testament. For the sake of this study, and following what has become a scholarly convention, I will call those who lived during the time of the Old Testament "Israelites" and their religion "Israelite religion," as opposed to the "Jews" and "Judaism" of the late biblical period and beyond.

In modern English, the term *Christian* (from the Greek word *christianos*, meaning "one belonging to Christ") suggests the existence of Christianity as a religion independent of Judaism, with its distinct set of religious beliefs and practices. There was no such form of Christianity during the time of the New Testament. The earliest followers of Jesus were Jews, like Jesus himself, and Christianity evolved to become its own religion only long after the time of Jesus. The term *Christian* is found three times in the New Testament (in Acts 11:26; 26:28; and 1 Peter 4:16). There it is used for the followers of Jesus, those who have come to believe that Jesus is the Messiah of Israel. The term has remained in use ever since. In the New Testament, it does not imply the existence of Christianity as its own religion, independent of Judaism, as we ordinarily use the term today. I will therefore call those in the New Testament who believed in

Jesus "followers of Jesus" and reserve the term "Christians" for the believers in postbiblical times.

The term *Old Testament* is the Christian designation for the first part of the Christian Bible. The Old Testament is a collection of ancient Jewish writings that the early Christians adopted from Judaism as sacred texts. These writings then became their Bible. As a matter of fact, for the followers of Jesus, this was their only Bible. The term *Old Testament* implies that there is a New Testament. Old Testament is therefore an exclusively Christian term. There are several terms that are used in Judaism to refer to these Jewish books. One of the more common terms is *Hebrew Bible*, which today is also widely used by biblical scholars. The term *Hebrew Bible* has the advantages that it is largely descriptive (it simply indicates that these writings were originally written in Hebrew) and that it does not privilege Christianity over Judaism.

When I use the term *Old Testament* in this book, I do not wish to exclude Jewish readers, even though I acknowledge that the term itself is exclusive. Rather, my intention is to highlight the singular importance the Jewish Scriptures have had for the followers of Jesus. To avoid the term *Old Testament* in an effort to be inclusive, as some Christians do today, misses the point that the Hebrew Bible is theologically relevant for Christians *only* in connection with the New Testament, regardless of what we call it. In other words, for Christians, the Hebrew Bible will always be the Old Testament.

It is a curious fact of the textual history of the Bible that the Old Testament exists in more than one form. In that regard, it is different from the Hebrew Bible in Judaism or the Qur'an in Islam, which have not changed in form over time. What are these different forms of the Old Testament? First, there is the Jewish Bible written in Hebrew. It is a collection of ancient Jewish books that are organized in three parts: the Torah (the five books of Moses, also called the Pentateuch), the Prophets, and the Writings. The Jewish Bible as it is used in synagogues today, and English translations of it, are all based on the original Hebrew text of the Old Testament. Second, there is the

Protestant Old Testament. It closely follows the Jewish Bible and includes the same books, but the order of the books is rearranged. Third, there is the Old Testament of the Roman Catholic Church and of several Orthodox Churches. It is based not on the Hebrew text of the Jewish Bible but on the translation of the Hebrew text into Greek, a version of the Bible known as the Septuagint (I will explain the origin and significance of the Septuagint in chapter 2). The Septuagint includes all the books of the Jewish Bible (and the Protestant Old Testament), but it also includes a number of additional books known today as the Apocrypha (from the Greek word *apokryphos*, meaning "hidden away; obscure; kept secret"). The Roman Catholic Old Testament is therefore more expansive than the Jewish Bible and Protestant Old Testament. The additional books in the Roman Catholic Old Testament all come from the Second Temple period (the sixth century BCE to the first century CE). Fourth and finally, a number of Orthodox Churches have Old Testaments that include even more books than the Roman Catholic Old Testament. The Ethiopian Orthodox Church, for example, includes books in its Old Testament that are not part of the Jewish and Protestant or of the Roman Catholic Bibles. Two books that are considered biblical in the Ethiopian Church are 1 Enoch and Jubilees. I will return to them later in the book. When I use the term *Old Testament* in this book, I refer to the Protestant Old Testament.

Finally, a word about methodology. Jesus himself did not write anything down. Nowhere in the New Testament are we told that Jesus sat down to record any of his own teachings. We do not have a single text that claims to be written by Jesus himself. All we have are texts *about Jesus* that were written by other authors who lived at a later time. There is a general consensus among biblical scholars, for example, that none of the four Gospel writers of the New Testament ever saw Jesus. It is possible, and even likely, that when they wrote their Gospels, the evangelists relied on eyewitness accounts and written sources that go back to the time of Jesus (see, for example, Luke 1:1–4). But the Gospels as we have them today in our Bible were most certainly written long after the life of Jesus.

Methodologically speaking, this means that we need to distinguish between what scholars call "the historical Jesus," that is, the Jesus of ancient Israel whom we hope to reconstruct through various forms of textual archaeology, and the Jesus who is described in the documents of the New Testament. The two are not the same. When reading the Gospel of Matthew, for example, how are we to determine which sayings actually come from Jesus and which Matthew may have added or changed? There can be little doubt that Matthew and, indeed, all the authors of the New Testament rearranged the material they in turn had received and have given it their own interpretation. When the four Gospels disagree with one another, as they often do, how do we know whose account is closest to the historical Jesus? In this book, I am not concerned with the historical Jesus. Rather, my focus will be on Jesus as we read about him in the four Gospels and in the letters of Paul. I acknowledge the importance of distinguishing between the historical Jesus and the Jesus of the New Testament. For the sake of this study, however, I am content to read the biblical books as we have received them, without making an effort to reach behind the texts in an attempt to reconstruct the historical Jesus.

Mind the Gap!

I have borrowed the title of this book, *Mind the Gap*, from the London Underground, or the Tube, as it is commonly known. I trust it won't mind. There, the phrase "Mind the Gap" cautions rail passengers who are about to board a train and directs their attention to the spatial gap between the station platform and the train door. The gap to which I am referring in this book is not a spatial gap. It is a *chronological* gap, a period of several hundred years in between the Old and the New Testament from which next to no books are preserved in the Protestant Bible.

A closer look at this gap reveals that this was a time of extra-

JJ ordinary creativity and great literary productivity in ancient
Israel. It just so happens that the books that were written during the time between the Testaments never became part of the
Jewish Bible (or, as a consequence, of the Protestant Old Testament), which explains in part why these ancient Jewish books
are equally unknown today to most modern Jews and Christians. My argument is that if we want to be serious about the
Judaism of Jesus and learn about it, we cannot ignore this time
and the rich literature it produced only because it is skipped
over in our Bibles. Even though commonly overlooked, these
books turn out to be indispensable, the only source we have
about the Judaism of Jesus apart from the New Testament.
These are the texts Schalom Ben-Chorin used when he taught
us about his "brother Jesus" in the lecture hall in Hanover.
When read together with the earliest accounts of Jesus in the
New Testament, these forgotten Jewish books succinctly capture and reveal to us the Jewish world of Jesus.

PART I

Mind the Gap! Reading between the Old and the New Testament

1

When Was the Old Testament Written? A Brief Timeline

The Bible is not a book that was written by a single author. It is a small library, a collection of diverse books that were written by different people, in different places, at different times, for different audiences, and even in different languages (the Old Testament was mostly written in Hebrew, with some passages in Aramaic, and the New Testament in Greek). When modern biblical scholarship developed as an academic discipline in the eighteenth and nineteenth centuries, scholars were poised to find out more about who wrote the books of the Bible, and where and when they were written. Since then, much progress has been made. Today, we are reasonably well informed about the history of the Bible and its main dates, even if many questions remain.

Before we look more closely at some of these dates and events, it is necessary to draw a distinction between the Old and the New Testament. Both Testaments were written over a significant period of time, but that period is much shorter for the New than it is for the Old Testament. The books of the New Testament were composed during the latter half of the first century CE. The apostle Paul, himself a Jew and, at the same time, the first Christian author ("Christian" in the sense of "follower of Jesus") whose texts have survived, wrote his letters in the 50s of the first century, roughly a couple of decades after the death of Jesus. His letters are the oldest Christian texts we have. The Gospels were written a few decades later, after the Roman destruction of Jerusalem in the year 70 CE. And the book of Revelation, the last book in the Christian Bible, dates from the end of the first century CE. That is, the New Testament was written in about fifty years, roughly in between the years 50 and 100 CE.

The books of the Old Testament, by contrast, span a much longer period. There is no consensus among scholars about the date of the oldest texts in the Old Testament. Most scholars will agree that some of the songs and poems that are now embedded in the biblical stories, such the Song of Miriam in Exodus 15, for example, the Song of Moses in Deuteronomy 32, and the Song of Deborah in Judges 5, are among the oldest texts in the Old Testament. These ancient poems may have been written as early as the eleventh or even the twelfth century BCE. We are on firmer ground when it comes to the dating of the youngest book in the Old Testament. That is the book of Daniel, which we can date with some confidence to the middle of the second century BCE. In sum, the books of the Old Testament cover a period of at least nine hundred years, from the eleventh to the second century BCE, and, if we pushed the date of the earliest texts back to the twelfth century, which I think is probable, possibly even a full millennium.

In this book, the focus will be on the Old Testament, and particularly on the latter period of its history, the time of the Second Temple.

This chapter consists of three parts. I begin with a very brief overview of the history of biblical Israel. A basic familiarity with its main dates and events will be necessary for placing the

2)

biblical books in their proper historical context. Next, I turn to some of the books in the Old Testament and briefly discuss their date of composition. Here the goal is twofold: first, to provide a general overview of when the books of the Old Testament were written, and second, to point out that there is *a sizeable time gap* between the Old and the New Testament, a period of several hundred years in the history of ancient Israel from which almost no books made it into the Christian Bibles (the situation is different in the case of the Septuagint, as I explain in the next chapter). The last books in the Old Testament were written in the fourth century BCE. Then there is the book of Daniel, which comes from the second century BCE.

With the New Testament, we jump to the first century CE. With the exception of the book of Daniel there is a gap of about four hundred years between the Testaments. This, of course, does not mean that Jewish scribes somehow stopped writing. Quite the opposite is true! The gap years between the Testaments were a time of intense literary activity in ancient Israel. It just happens that the Old Testament includes hardly any of these texts. The Old Testament is *not* a complete collection of all the writings that were produced in ancient Israel—far from it. Jewish scribes continued to write books, books that never became part of the Jewish or Protestant Bibles. I will return to some of these forgotten writings from the gap years and introduce them in greater detail in the next chapter.

3) In the third part of the chapter, finally, I turn briefly to the arrangement of the biblical books in the Old Testament. Normally we may not pay much attention to the canonical order in which the books appear in the Old Testament. But their order does matter. The books have been arranged carefully, and their arrangement has profound implications for how we think about the connection between the Old and the New Testament, perhaps more so than many of us are aware. The last book in the Protestant Old Testament is the book of the prophet Malachi. It ends with an eschatological prophecy about the end of time. From there, the reader of the Protestant Bible moves directly to the first book in the New Testament, which is the Gospel of Matthew. Matthew begins with a genealogy of Jesus, a genealogy whose purpose it is to trace Jesus's ancestry all the way back to Abraham and, at the same time, to demonstrate, generation by generation, how deeply Jesus is rooted in the Old Testament. Theologically, then, there is a very close connection between the Old and the New Testament: the reader moves seamlessly from the biblical prophets to the birth of Jesus, or from prophetic promise to messianic fulfillment. Chronologically, however, the transition is not so seamless. No less than half a millennium of Jewish history elapsed in between Malachi and Matthew, a long period during which the religion and literature of ancient Israel changed in significant ways that are of great importance for our understanding of the world of Jesus.

A Brief Sketch of the History of Ancient Israel

The history of ancient Israel is divided by what was arguably its most traumatic event, the destruction of Jerusalem and the Jerusalem temple by the Neo-Babylonian king Nebuchadnezzar II. In 597 BCE, King Nebuchadnezzar marched against Jerusalem, conquered the city, plundered the temple, and put a puppet king whom he named Zedekiah on the throne. When a decade later Zedekiah revolted against Nebuchadnezzar, the Babylonian king swiftly returned to Jerusalem, took the city again, this time destroyed its temple, and deported the educated and wealthy parts of the Judean population into exile in Babylon. All of this happened in the year 587 BCE. The Babylonian exile, as it came to be known, lasted for about half a century until the Babylonians themselves were defeated by the Persians, another ancient Near Eastern superpower. In 539 BCE, the Persian king Cyrus the Great was able to conquer the city of Babylon, apparently without much resistance, and brought an end to the Babylonian Empire. Whereas the Babylonians were ruthless conquerors who pillaged whatever civilization was in their way, the Persians treated their subject nations with more respect. They allowed the people the Babylonians had exiled to return home and rebuild their lives and sanctuaries, among them the Israelites. Thus, the Babylonian exile, which began in 587 BCE when Nebuchadnezzar destroyed Jerusalem, came to an end with King Cyrus, who in 538 BCE, only one year after he had conquered the city of Babylon, issued a proclamation allowing the Israelites to return to Jerusalem and rebuild their temple. Many of them did, and in 515 BCE, after some delays, the Second Temple was built and rededicated in Jerusalem.

When scholars speak about the history of ancient Israel, the first distinction they make is between the preexilic period (Israel's history prior to the year 587 BCE), the exilic period, or simply the Babylonian exile (the years 587–538 BCE), and the postexilic period (the years after 538 BCE). The Babylonian exile separates the First from the Second Temple period. The First Temple was built by King Solomon, son and successor of King David, who reigned in Jerusalem in the tenth century BCE. The temple served as the religious center of Israel's worship, where the high priests resided and the Israelites brought their sacrificial offerings. It was also the place where the ark of the covenant was kept and where the glory of God resided, assuring the Israelites of the protective presence of their God in their midst (1 Kings 8). The First Temple period lasted from the tenth to the sixth century BCE, when the Solomonic temple was destroyed by the Babylonians. The rededication of the Second Temple in March 515 BCE marked the beginning of the Second Temple period. It lasted for nearly six centuries, until the Second Temple was destroyed by the Romans in the year 70 CE. The most significant part of the larger Second Temple complex that has survived to this day is the Western Wall, a segment of the retaining wall at the southwestern edge of the Temple Mount built by King Herod. The Western Wall remains of great significance for Jews today. Since 70 CE, there has not been a temple in Judaism, in Jerusalem or elsewhere.

A Brief Timeline of the Bible

The Old Testament
(Second Temple Period)

The New Testament

Ancient Jewish Literature

539 BCE	332 BCE	164 BCE	63 BCE	70 CE
Persian Period	Hellenistic Period	Maccabean Period	Roman Period	Jerusalem destroyed

The Torah / Five Books of Moses (5th/4th cent. BCE)

Haggai (525 BCE)
Isaiah 56–66 (after 515 BCE)
Malachi (5th cent. BCE)

Ezra/Nehemiah (4th cent. BCE)
1 and 2 Chronicles (4th cent. BCE)
Esther (4th cent. BCE)
Qohelet (4th cent. BCE)

Daniel (167–164 BCE)

The Septuagint (LXX)
The Dead Sea Scrolls (3rd cent. BCE–68 CE)

Book of the Watchers (300 BCE)

Jubilees (mid-2nd cent. BCE)

Psalms of Solomon (post-63 BCE)

Apostle Paul (ca. 50s)
The Gospels (ca. 70–100 CE)

2 Baruch/
4 Ezra (late 1st cent. CE)

The focus of this overview is on the Second Temple period, and particularly on its last centuries, an often overlooked and yet altogether remarkable time in the history of Israel. The roughly six hundred years that make up the Second Temple period can further be divided into four distinct eras (see the timeline). It is important to keep them apart, not only because of the historical changes that came with each era, but also because each era produced its own set of Jewish writings that reflect and often directly respond to these changes.

The first of the four eras is the Persian period, which lasted about two hundred years (539–332 BCE). It began, as already mentioned, when King Cyrus the Great overthrew the Babylonian Empire and allowed the exiles to return home. Cyrus issued a decree ordering the rebuilding of the Jerusalem temple. It is impossible to say whether the words of the decree preserved in the Bible are Cyrus's actual words (see Ezra 1:1–4; 6:1–5). We do know, however, of an archaeological artifact that gives us some information about this period. This is the famous Cyrus Cylinder, an ancient clay cylinder from the time of Cyrus that has an inscription written on its surface. In the inscription, which is written in Akkadian cuneiform script, Cyrus relates how he took the city of Babylon and allowed the conquered nations to return home. The Israelites are not mentioned in the inscription, but what Cyrus claims in his cylinder is remarkably similar to what we read about him in the Bible. While many of the Israelites who lived in exile in Babylon followed Cyrus's ordinance and returned home to Judah, a portion of the exiles decided to stay in Babylonia. In later centuries, their numbers grew into a significant Jewish diaspora community, with much influence on Jewish life and culture (the Greek word *diaspora* means "a scattering"; diaspora therefore means the dispersion of Jewish communities outside the land of Israel). The biblical account focuses on those who returned to Jerusalem, however. Their primary task was to rebuild their lives at home. Progress was slowed by ongoing conflicts between those who had been in exile and those who had remained in the land. Restoration happened on many levels. The physical restoration of the city of Jerusalem involved the rebuilding of the city and its walls. The religious restoration focused on the building and rededication of the Second Temple. And the social restoration involved difficult debates over what it meant to be a Judean, which was increasingly understood in religious as opposed to national terms. The Persian period was also a creative time when some of the last books that are included in the Old Testament were written. I return to the biblical literature from the Persian period in the next section.

2nd   The second era of the Second Temple period is the Hel-
Era   lenistic period (332–63 BCE). The term Hellenistic derives from the Greek word *hellen,* meaning "Greek." The Hellenistic, or Greek, period began with the brilliant Macedonian-Greek king Alexander the Great (356–323 BCE), who defeated the Persians and built a vast Greek kingdom that included Mesopotamia and reached all the way to India. When in 333/332 BCE Alexander conquered Asia Minor and the land of Israel, Jerusalem surrendered and was therefore spared destruction. After Alexander's death in 323 BCE at the age of thirty-three, his enormous kingdom broke apart and was divided, and a long struggle ensued among Alexander's generals. From 301 BCE onward, Judea with its capital Jerusalem was part of the kingdom of Egypt (under the rule of the Ptolemies, so named after a Greek general, Ptolemy, who established the Ptolemaic dynasty in Egypt), but in 200 BCE, Judea was conquered by the kingdom of Syria (under the Seleucids, founded by Seleucus I Nicator, another Greek general who had previously served under Alexander). This meant that throughout the Hellenistic period, the Israelites lived in the shadow of different Greek rulers.

What makes the Hellenistic period so important is the enormous cultural and religious influence that the Greeks had on their subject nations, including the Jews. Scholars refer to this phenomenon as Hellenism, or Hellenization. By this they mean the advancement of the Greek language, culture, religion, lifestyle, and politics that began with Alexander the Great in the fourth century BCE and lasted in some form for over a millennium until the Arab conquests of the seventh century

CE. Greek domination meant that the common language was Greek, social customs and literature were Greek, and the religion was Greek. Hellenism was a way of life that was imposed on all who were living under Greek rule. This posed some major challenges for the Jews: the question was not whether or not to adopt the Greek language and lifestyle—that was simply a given. Rather, the challenge for the Jews during the Hellenistic period, both in Israel and in the diaspora, was to determine how much to become Hellenized while still being truthful to their own roots and Jewish identity. This was the great challenge for Hellenistic Judaism: for the Jews who lived during the Hellenistic period to find ways of incorporating those aspects of Hellenistic culture into their own lives that they considered compatible with their own religion, without compromising their Jewish identity.

The Persian and Hellenistic periods were largely peaceful, without any major uprisings. This changed in the 160s BCE, when a massive conflict erupted between a certain Seleucid (that is, Greek-Syrian) king named Antiochus IV Epiphanes (175–164 BCE; his name means "god manifest") and the Jews living in Judea. The exact events leading up to the conflict are not entirely clear. What is clear, however, is that in 167 BCE Antiochus, who was an aggressive proponent of Greek culture, turned his attention to Jerusalem, plundered the temple, erected an altar for Zeus Olympius in the Jerusalem temple, and brought a sacrifice to the Greek god. In addition to desecrating the temple, Antiochus outlawed many of the traditional practices of Judaism, such as circumcision and observing the Sabbath. Not all Jews were opposed to Antiochus, however. Jason, for example, who was the high priest in Jerusalem at the time of Antiochus, built a gymnasium in Jerusalem that was frequented by many Jews (2 Maccabees 4:7–17). Such Jewish collaboration with Antiochus only energized the opposition to Antiochus further. Before long, his persecution of the Jews led to an armed resistance known as the Maccabean revolt. The family that led the revolt is variously known as the Hasmoneans or the Maccabees. Their father was a certain Mattathias, a priest from the city of Modein, whose sons, Judas Maccabeus, Jonathan, Simon, John, and Eleazar, continued to build the Maccabean dynasty. In 164 BCE, Judas managed to regain control of the Jerusalem temple. The rededication of the Second Temple in the same year is commemorated in the Jewish festival of Hanukkah. For the next century (164–63 BCE), Judea was ruled by the Hasmonean family, whose members assumed the offices of both the kingship and the high priesthood. Strictly speaking, this third era, the Maccabean period, is not a distinct period, since it did not replace the Hellenistic period. And yet, things changed significantly for the inhabitants of Judea. A couple of decades after the Maccabean revolt, the Seleucid rulers were forced to accept the independence of the Maccabean kingdom. What began as a revolt by a priestly family against Antiochus's profanation of the temple and the persecution of the Jews turned into the establishment of an independent Jewish state, at least for a century.

The fourth and final era of the Second Temple period is the Roman period. In 63 BCE Pompey conquered Jerusalem and incorporated Judea into the Roman Empire. Pompey's conquest was facilitated by a certain amount of infighting among the Hasmoneans. In any event, Pompey's victory meant the end of Jewish independence and the inauguration of the Roman period. In the year 70 CE, the Romans under the leadership of Titus suppressed a Jewish revolt and destroyed the temple in Jerusalem. Even though the temple now lay in ruins never to be rebuilt again, the Second Temple period was not quite over. In 132 to 135 CE, the region saw a final Jewish uprising against Roman rule. The Bar Kokhba revolt, so called after its leader (his name means "son of the star"), was a last failed attempt to break free from Roman domination and to regain control over Judea. The Romans were quick to suppress the revolt, which meant that the Second Temple period was finally over.

Judaism of the Second Temple period was diverse and multifaceted. The political landscape shifted constantly from the Persian to the Hellenistic, Maccabean, and finally the Roman period. At no point was Judaism a single, homogeneous group that was governed by a single set of rules. Judaism *always* consisted of different groups, each with its own religious beliefs and practices. Whenever we attempt to understand the Jewish world of Jesus, it is imperative to avoid the simplified cliché of a monolithic Judaism and instead to recognize that early Judaism was as vibrant as it was complex.

When Was the Old Testament Written?

With this rough overview of the history of the Second Temple period in mind, we can now turn to the compositional dates of the biblical books. I begin with the Torah, the five books of Moses. For a long time, scholars argued that the Torah reached its present form during the Babylonian exile. The assumption was that, much like the Bible as a whole, the Torah grew together over several centuries out of previously independent sources. That process of gradual growth reached its end during the Babylonian exile, when the ancient scribes collected the written materials from the preexilic period and put them together to compile the Torah as we have it today. In recent decades, a growing number of scholars has questioned that model, or at least its dates. While there is little doubt that the Torah was put together out of different sources stemming from the First Temple period, many scholars now argue that the process of formation extended beyond the exile into the fifth, and some would even say the fourth century BCE, that is, into the Persian period. By that time, the Torah was completed.

The situation with the prophets is similar. The books of the major prophets—Isaiah, Jeremiah, and Ezekiel—were completed not long after the Babylonian exile. The last chapters of the book of Isaiah, chapters 55–56, are commonly dated to the last decades of the sixth century BCE, after the exiles had returned home. The prophet Haggai, who dates from the year 525 BCE, writes of the delays in the rebuilding of the Second Temple in Jerusalem. And the last of the prophets, Malachi, whose book was written a few decades after the rededication of the Second Temple, is highly critical of the way the new temple is run by the priests. With Malachi, the writing of prophetic books in ancient Israel came to a close.

Then there is a group of Old Testament books that are commonly dated to the fourth century. Among them are the books of Ezra and Nehemiah, two of the main figures of the restoration. Ezra was a priest and a scribe who led a wave of returnees from Babylonia to Jerusalem. Nehemiah 8 tells the story of how Ezra arrived in Jerusalem and, standing on an enormous wooden platform, read the Torah of Moses to a large public gathering. In Judaism, Ezra is thus revered as the scribe who gave the Torah to the returnees, interpreted it for them, and presided over the people's recommitment to its stipulations. Nehemiah played a different role. He was in charge of the repopulation of Jerusalem, the building of the city walls, and the implementation of numerous religious reforms. Ezra and Nehemiah were both active in the middle of the fifth century BCE, but many scholars believe that the books that are named after them may not have been written until the fourth century BCE.

First and Second Chronicles are a retelling of the biblical story, beginning with Adam and concluding with the declaration of the Persian king Cyrus in 538 BCE allowing the exiled nation to return home. The bulk of the material in Chronicles recasts the books of Samuel and Kings, the time in Israel's history from the Judges to the end of the Babylonian exile. The authors of 1 and 2 Chronicles felt rather free in their treatment of the biblical texts. They omitted much of the source materials, added more, and rewrote significant sections. This process of rewriting the biblical story is a very early form of biblical interpretation that enabled its authors to express their own theological perspectives and concerns while imbuing the biblical text with new meaning. It is difficult to know with certainty when 1 and 2 Chronicles were written, though a date during the Persian period seems most likely.

The book of Esther tells the story of a young Jewish orphan who ascends in rank to become the queen of Persia, where, together with her cousin Mordecai, she narrowly averts a massacre of the Jews of the eastern diaspora. The book is centered solely on the life of the Jews in the East, and the land of Israel and the Jerusalem temple are not even mentioned. It therefore seems likely that Esther was written in the eastern diaspora, probably toward the end of the Persian period. Finally, Ecclesiastes (meaning "the one who assembles"), also known as Qoheleth, is a very different kind of book. Whereas 1 and 2 Chronicles could fall under the broad category of Jewish history, and Esther could be labeled a diaspora tale, Qoheleth belongs to the wisdom books in the Bible. That is, it contains a personal reflection by a man named Qoheleth on the nature of the world, on God who made and controls it, and on the fate of human beings in the world. The sage, who speaks in the first person singular, covers a range of topics, including the cycles of the natural order, the conception of time (the book may be best known for the poem in Qoheleth chapter 3), the enjoyment that comes from one's toil, the frustration that comes from the limitations of human wisdom, and life's ever-present uncertainties, most of all death. Qoheleth's date of composition has been debated, with some arguing for a date in the Hellenistic period, while others opt for the late Persian period. Some of the biblical Psalms, Proverbs, and the Song of Solomon are sometimes dated to the Persian period as well, but in all of these cases the actual date of composition is much less clear.

The youngest book to be included in the Old Testament is the book of Daniel. The book falls into two halves of roughly equal length but of different literary character and origin. Chapters 1–6 are composed of six stories *about* Daniel and his three companions, who, not unlike Queen Esther, rise through the ranks at the courts of foreign monarchs. These tales are followed in chapters 7–12 by a sequence of four apocalyptic visions by Daniel. The stories in the first half of Daniel are concerned with the lives of the Jews in the diaspora. They were almost certainly written in the diaspora and reflect on the challenges faced by the Jews who are living outside the land of Israel. Their date of composition is uncertain, though the third century BCE is a possibility. The apocalyptic visions in Daniel 7–12 reflect a rather different, considerably more hostile situation. Here, the foreign empires have turned from relatively hospitable host nations (Daniel 1–6) into apocalyptic beasts that rise from the sea (Daniel 7). Because apocalyptic authors in general, and the authors of Daniel 7–12 in particular, work specific allusions to their present-day circumstances into their visions, we can safely date these latter chapters in Daniel toward the end of the Maccabean revolt. The apocalyptic visions were written in response to the Jewish persecutions under Antiochus IV Epiphanes in 167–164 BCE.

To conclude, the last biblical books that provide us with some information about life in the land of Israel are Ezra and Nehemiah. They pick up the story line where 2 Chronicles ends, with King Cyrus's decree of return (compare 2 Chronicles 36:22–23 with Ezra 1:2–4). The restoration and religious reforms outlined in Ezra and Nehemiah date from the fifth century BCE. This marks the very beginning of the Second Temple period. Esther is set in the Persian period, toward the beginning of the Second Temple period. Like Daniel 1–6, it reflects a new reality of ancient Israel, Jewish life in the diaspora, and shows no interest in the land of Israel. Qoheleth, finally, may date from the middle of the Second Temple period, the late Persian or possibly early Hellenistic period. The book is of particular interest to those who study ancient wisdom literature and its transformation through time, but it tells us very little, if anything, about life in postexilic Israel. The Protestant Old Testament includes no writings from the third, second, and first centuries BCE (with the exception of the book of Daniel). That is, Jewish writings from the latter half of the Second Temple period are conspicuous for their absence from the Old Testament, even though there were many. I will return to some of them in the next chapter.

From the Old Testament to the New: The Arrangement of the Books in the Protestant Bible

There is some variation in the order in which the books are

arranged in the biblical manuscripts, particularly in the manuscripts of the Greek translation of the Old Testament known as the Septuagint. The last book in the Protestant Old Testament is the prophetic book of Malachi. From there, the Christian reader goes straight to the Gospel of Matthew, the first book in the New Testament. Malachi ends with a prophetic announcement of the great day when the Lord will defeat the wicked and reward the righteous. "See, the day is coming, burning like an oven, when all the arrogant and all evildoers will be stubble. . . . But for you who revere my name the sun of righteousness shall rise" (Malachi 4:1–2). At the time of the end, God will send the prophet Elijah, the herald of the messianic age, to bring about reconciliation among the generations and to prepare Israel for that great and terrible day. Such an eschatological ending is a fitting conclusion to the writings of the prophets. Some scholars have even suggested that these final verses were added later to Malachi as a secondary conclusion to the corpus of prophetic books in the Bible. The Gospel of Matthew explicitly draws on Malachi 3:1 and 4:1 and identifies John the Baptist with Elijah: in the Gospel of Matthew, John the Baptist has taken on the role of Elijah as the precursor of the messiah (see Matthew 3:1–2; 11:2–15; and especially 17:12). The reader thus moves effortlessly from the prophetic announcement of the end of time and the return of Elijah at the end of the Old Testament to the genealogy and birth of Jesus the Messiah at the beginning of the New Testament.

Theologically, this arrangement makes good sense and creates a smooth transition from ancient Israel to the origin of Christianity. The concept of promise and fulfillment is an effective and theologically important way of connecting the two Testaments. The same connection between prophecy and Jesus is made throughout the Gospel of Matthew. Matthew frequently refers back to the prophetic writings of the Old Testament, quotes specific passages, and emphasizes that what has been promised by the prophets of old has come true in the life of Jesus (see Matthew 1:22–23; 2:5–6, 15, 17–18, and many more examples). Moreover, Matthew's portrait of Jesus is closely modeled after that of the biblical prophets, and especially after that of Moses. Deuteronomy already makes clear that the foremost qualification of any prophet in Israel was that he should be "like Moses" (Deuteronomy 18:15–22; 34:10). Matthew thus reinforces even further the close ties between the Old Testament prophets and Jesus. All of this is intended to connect Jesus to Israel's past and, specifically, to ground Jesus in Israel's prophetic tradition. It creates the impression that Jesus emerged directly from among Israel's prophets, whose tradition he continues.

Chronologically, however, we need to bear in mind that by turning the page, the reader of the Bible leaps from the fifth century BCE, the time of Malachi, straight to the first century CE, the date of composition of the Gospel of Matthew. Malachi and Matthew are separated by a chronological gap of no less than half a millennium. In the following chapter, we will take a closer look at this gap and examine the rich literature that was composed during that period.

2

———

Ancient Judaism and Its Literatures

Mind the Gap!

We noted in the previous chapter that there is a significant chronological gap between the Old and the New Testament. With the exception of the book of Daniel, the Protestant Bible does not include any books that were written in between the fourth century BCE and the first century CE. In other words, there is a period of about four hundred years that is absent from the Protestant Bible. We are justified in calling these the dark centuries of biblical literature, because the reader of the Bible learns next to nothing about them; they are simply glossed over and missing from the biblical record.

Today, we fortunately do have access to a significant number of texts that have come down to us from that period. These ancient Jewish books provide a great wealth of information about the years in between the Old and the New Testament. The picture that emerges from them is anything but dark. This was the time in ancient Israel when professionally trained scribes played an increasingly important role. They were lay people who were deeply learned and schooled in the sacred traditions. These ancient scribes devoted great care to the preservation and transmission of the old texts, the books that eventually became the Old Testament. They copied and disseminated the ancient books. And they began to interpret them. As the old texts became authoritative and the communities of the faithful turned to them in search of meaning, the need arose to interpret the sacred texts. Any text that becomes authoritative will at some point be in need of interpretation.

But the scribes did more than caring for, transmitting, and interpreting the old texts—they also produced a wealth of new books, the rich literature of Second Temple Judaism. As we saw in the previous chapter, these new texts are not well known today, among Jews or Christians, because they never became part of Jewish and Protestant Bibles. Since relatively little attention was devoted to them, they were largely forgotten for two millennia in the West until they were rediscovered in the nineteenth and early twentieth centuries. Today, these texts are increasingly recognized and studied in their own right, and they are beginning to change the way we think about ancient Judaism, Jesus, and the early Jesus movement.

reasons to pay attention — There are a number of reasons why we need to pay attention to the scribal activities during the gap years between the Testaments. First, and perhaps most obviously, the Bible has only preserved a fraction of the Jewish literature that was produced and circulated in ancient Judaism. Even though many of us will only be familiar with the Bible, this does not mean that the Bible contains all the literature there was in ancient Israel. In addition to the familiar biblical books, there were several other texts that were written at the time. Many of the books that remained outside the Bible were of crucial importance for different Jewish groups.

2) A second reason why we need to pay attention to the gap years is that the oldest manuscripts of the Old Testament come from this period. These manuscripts were discovered among the Dead Sea Scrolls, and they provide invaluable information about the textual history of the Bible. Whereas prior to the dis-

covery of the Dead Sea Scrolls in the 1940s and 1950s there was little hope that we would ever be able to reach back to the earliest stages in the formation of the Bible, now with the Dead Sea Scrolls we have access to invaluable information about how the Bible came to be.

3) Third, the Second Temple texts tell us a great deal about pre-Christian Judaism. They testify to a Judaism that was heavily fragmented and broken up into smaller groups, sects, and alliances. All of these diverse groups claimed that they were descendants from the ancient Israelites, but they also had their significant differences with one another. Writing texts was one way for them to claim their authority and to explain how their religious beliefs and practices differed from those of the others. For us today, the literature they produced opens a window into this fascinating period of intense Jewish debate and wrangling over a host of issues. Their texts illustrate how many new themes and topics entered the discourse, and how these issues were widely and vigorously debated.

There is a long list of religious topics that we might think today have been debated in Judaism since biblical times. But a closer look reveals that we find either very little or no discussion of them at all in the Old Testament. It was only during the gap years that these topics became a prominent part of the religious discourse. Such topics include the expectation of *a* a messiah, a divine agent who will come at the end of time to bring about the restoration of Israel; an interest in cosmol- *b* ogy, demons, and unclean spirits; a focus on the Torah as the *c* rule book that defines Jewish practice and identity; a concern *d* about what will happen to humans after we die; and the hope *ε* for the resurrection of the dead and the afterlife (again, we would expect the Old Testament to be filled with texts that talk about life after death, but for some reason the biblical authors stopped short of speculating about what will happen to us after we die). These topics, and others could be added, all have in common that they are virtually absent from the Old Testament but emerged during the late Second Temple period and quickly moved to the center of the religious debates. They have been part of Judaism ever since.

By the time of Jesus, the religion of ancient Israel had evolved. This was no longer the time of the Old Testament, this was now the time of late Second Temple Judaism. Jesus was not immersed in the religion of the ancient Israelites as it is described in the Old Testament, he was part of first-century Judaism. Of course, there is no absolute break between Israelite religion and early Judaism. Both share a belief in the one God, who created heaven and earth, who called Abraham, who elected the Israelites as his chosen people, who entered into a covenant with them, and who gave them the Torah. And both emphasize a special tie to the land of Israel and, particularly, to the city of Jerusalem. But over time, Judaism underwent a number of changes, and by the first century CE, the religious landscape was not the same anymore.

Reading through the Gospels, we find Jesus deeply absorbed in the religious debates of his time. He is concerned about messianic expectations, he expels demons, he expounds the Torah in conversation with the Pharisees, he preaches about the end of time, he looks forward to the resurrection of the dead, and he discusses life after death with the Sadducees. To the modern reader of the New Testament who tries to make sense of Jesus's words on the background of the Old Testament alone, Jesus must seem radical, since what he says does not really resemble much of what we read in the Old Testament. But when we put Jesus in his appropriate historical and religious context—Judaism of first-century Israel—we begin to understand many things: that Jesus is part of a much larger world that is assumed in the New Testament but never fully explained, that Jesus participates in an ongoing religious debate that is much larger than the New Testament, and that many of the very issues Jesus debates and preaches are being debated and preached (and, in fact, have been debated and preached for centuries) by many other groups and religious authorities as well. Context matters. The Old Testament will not give us the context that can explain the Judaism of Jesus.

For that we need to read beyond the Bible and consider the books that were written during the time in between the Old and the New Testament. In a word, to understand the Jewish world of Jesus, we need to "Mind the Gap."

What is the gap? The gap is an empty space in the literary record of the Protestant Bible. The gap is a lacuna of roughly four hundred years from which there are no books in the Christian Bible (with the exception of the book of Daniel). How did this gap come about? The gap is the result of the making of the Bible. The books that are included in the Hebrew and Protestant Bibles do not include much of the late Second Temple literature. Undoubtedly, the making of the Bible, or what scholars call the canonical process, was much more complicated than a group of religious authorities sitting around a table and determining which books would be included in the Bible and which books would not. The list of books that ultimately came to be included in the Bible grew steadily over time. The result of the complicated process of this gradual literary growth is a Bible that omits close to half a millennium of early Jewish literature. Of course, Judaism continued to evolve during that time, and Jewish communities flourished in many places, both inside and outside of Israel. In fact, scribes were extraordinarily active during this time. Historically speaking, then, there is no gap. Jewish communities were thriving, scribes continued to transmit old texts and to compose new ones, and Judaism evolved rapidly. The gap is a literary phenomenon of the Protestant Bible; it is *not* a historical phenomenon of ancient Israel. It exists only in the literary record of the Protestant Bible—which, as we have seen, is far from complete. *There is no gap in the history, religion, and literature of ancient Israel!*

The purpose of this chapter is twofold. Its primary aim is to introduce a small sample of Jewish texts written during the gap years that may not be familiar to the reader. These texts only represent a fraction of the vast Jewish literature of the late Second Temple period, and other texts could be added that would be just as worthy of our attention. I have chosen these particular texts because of their significance for our understanding of early Judaism and the early Jesus movement. I will come back to all of them in the next four chapters and work with specific passages. The <u>second aim</u> of this chapter is <u>to showcase some of the new literary features and techniques that were introduced by the ingenious scribes of the Second Temple period.</u> True masters of their profession, these scribes were not shy about expanding the literary toolbox they had inherited from their biblical ancestors. Many of the books they wrote are modelled after the books of the Bible, a clear indication that they recognized and valued the normative authority of the Jewish Scriptures. But at the same time, they also went beyond the traditional literary conventions and introduced new writing styles and literary genres. New religious ideas called for new literary forms of expression.

Reading between the Testaments:
Ancient Judaism and Its Literatures

Ancient Jewish books are not always easy to understand, especially for the modern reader who may never have read them before. They are different from the biblical texts and therefore can be difficult to comprehend. With some explanation, however, the long-forgotten writings of ancient Judaism will come back to life. What initially may seem puzzling, strange, or awkward quickly becomes fascinating, rich, and relevant. When we study the ancient Jewish writings outside the Bible, we get a glimpse of *what was possible in early Judaism*. The courage with which these early Jewish thinkers of the late Second Temple period explored new religious concepts, thought new thoughts, and wrote new texts is truly remarkable. <u>The emergence of Jesus and his followers into a movement that a few centuries later became Christianity would have been unthinkable without the Jewish writers of the late Second Temple era.</u>

The Dead Sea Scrolls

The primary task of the scribes during the Second Temple period was the preservation of the old texts and the production of new texts. A splendid example of some of their work comes down to us from what is arguably the most important manuscript discovery of the twentieth century, the discovery of the Dead Sea Scrolls. The Dead Sea Scrolls are ancient Jewish manuscripts that were found in the Judean Desert along the northwestern shore of the Dead Sea. In the winter of 1946/47 a young Bedouin discovered a cave with seven ancient scrolls in it. Over the next decade, a total of eleven caves with manuscript remains were found in the area. Archaeologists also excavated a small settlement in the vicinity of the caves at a place called Qumran. Because of pottery that was found both in the settlement and in the caves, it is now clear that the scrolls belonged to the people who lived in the settlement at Qumran.

Qumran was a small Jewish community with anywhere between one and three hundred members. The archaeologists who excavated the settlement determined that the ruins did not resemble private residential units but most likely served as a communal center, with meeting places and a dining area. They also identified one large rectangular room as the scriptorium, the place where some of the original Dead Sea Scrolls may have been written. Today, most scholars believe that the people at Qumran were an offshoot of a group called the Essenes. The Essenes were one of the Jewish groups described by several ancient authors, including Josephus, Pliny, and Philo, though they are never mentioned in the Qumran texts themselves. The Essenes were known for their strict lifestyle, characterized by their tightly knit communities, the sharing of communal property, their avoidance of wealth, their strict obedience and deference to their elders, and a hierarchy in their communities—all characteristics we also find articulated in the texts from Qumran in which the community describes itself. The community that left us the scrolls most likely moved into the area in the latter half of the second century BCE, and their settlement was destroyed by the Romans in the year 68 CE, so it existed for about two hundred years.

The total number of manuscripts found in the eleven caves in and around Qumran is approximately nine hundred. Some of the texts are well preserved. For example, one of the original scrolls from cave 1 is the large Isaiah scroll, which measures 734 cm (just over 24 feet) and contains all 66 chapters of the biblical book of Isaiah. A copy of it can be seen today in the Shrine of the Book, a special section of the Israel Museum in Jerusalem. But most of the scrolls are heavily damaged and have fallen into decay, with some of them no larger than the palm of a hand or a postage stamp. The majority of the manuscripts are parts of ancient scrolls, strips of parchment (parchment is animal skin that was specially prepared to serve as a smooth writing surface). Pieces of parchment were then sewn together, and the scroll was rolled up. The text is written in black ink directly onto the parchment. Most of the Dead Sea Scrolls are written in Hebrew and Aramaic, though some texts are written in Greek. The dates of the scrolls vary. The bulk of them were written over a period of three hundred years, from the second century BCE to the first century CE. Some of the scrolls are thus older than the community itself. That means that they must have been brought there from somewhere else.

What are the Dead Sea Scrolls all about? Roughly a quarter of the scrolls are copies of biblical books. Manuscripts of all of the books of the Old Testament were found among the scrolls with the exception of the book of Esther. Most biblical books are attested in multiple copies. These are the oldest biblical manuscripts that are known to exist. In addition to the biblical manuscripts, the scrolls include several major works that are interpretations of the Bible, while others talk about the life of the community, its leadership, its organization, and its beliefs. There are also a number of liturgical texts, poems and thanksgiving hymns, texts that explain the Qumran calendar, and apocalyptic compositions that predict what will happen at the end of time.

The Dead Sea Scrolls are particularly important for us

because they provide invaluable information about Judaism at the turn of the Common Era. There are two aspects in particular we need to bear in mind. First, not all texts that were found at Qumran were also written there. We now know for certain that a sizeable number of manuscripts were brought to Qumran from other places in Israel. This means that not all of the Dead Sea Scrolls reflect the thinking of the Qumran community. It also makes the discovery of the Qumran library all the more significant. What was found in the vicinity of the Dead Sea is not the accidental library of a relatively small splinter group. Rather, the Dead Sea Scrolls open up a window into the Jewish literature that circulated widely in ancient Israel and capture the thinking of more than just this group. And second, it is important to emphasize that the Dead Sea Scrolls are not Christian texts, as some have tried to claim. The Dead Sea Scrolls are Jewish manuscripts. No Christian texts were found among the Dead Sea Scrolls. There is nothing to suggest that the members of the Qumran community even knew of Jesus or of any of his followers, and none of the figures of the New Testament are mentioned in any of the scrolls. Still, the Dead Sea Scrolls are extremely valuable for our understanding of Jesus and the early Jesus movement, even if Jesus or his followers are never mentioned in them. The scrolls dramatically increase our knowledge of ancient Judaism, and they shed much light on the different Jewish groups and their beliefs and practices during pre-Christian times. More specifically, in several cases, the use of specific language in the New Testament Gospels is strikingly similar to the language we find in the scrolls, so much so that some scholars have wondered whether the evangelists knew of these Jewish beliefs and possibly even of the texts found at Qumran. To gain clarity on this issue, we will look at some specific examples.

The Septuagint

The scribes of the Second Temple period were copyists and preservers of the revered texts. They were also their first translators. The first translation of the Jewish Scriptures is called the Septuagint. An ancient Jewish text known as the Letter of Aristeas tells the story of its origin. It relates how the Greek king Ptolemy II Philadelphus wanted to include a copy of the Torah in his enormous library in Alexandria, Egypt. So, he invited seventy-two elders from Jerusalem to come to Egypt to prepare a Greek translation of the Hebrew Torah. When the men arrived from Jerusalem, they were warmly welcomed. They quickly completed their task of translation, and the result pleased the king so much that it was strictly forbidden to make any changes to the new translation. According to the Letter of Aristeas, all of this happened in the third century BCE.

Today the story, delightful as it is, is widely thought to be fictitious. The name Septuagint, however, from the Latin word *septuaginta*, meaning "seventy" (since some other ancient sources mention seventy instead of seventy-two translators), remains. Originally, the term Septuagint only meant the Greek translation of the Torah, as, for example, in the Letter of Aristeas, but eventually it was used to designate the Greek translation of *all* the books in the Old Testament, and finally even of some books that were not translations at all. It has also become clear that the project of translating the Hebrew text into Greek began in the third century BCE in Alexandria, Egypt, but then continued during the following centuries and involved more translators in other locations, probably including ancient Israel.

Why is the Septuagint significant? Several answers can be given. First, the fact that there was a need for the Hebrew Scriptures to be translated into Greek as early as the third century BCE proves the enormous influence that the Greek language and culture had on the Jews living in Egypt, Israel, and the diaspora. Following the reign of Alexander the Great (336–323 BCE) and his conquest of Asia Minor (including Israel), Hellenism, or the advancement of the Greek language, culture, politics, and lifestyle, spread throughout the enormous empire Alexander had built. Jews, too, became part of Greek culture, and some of them, especially those living outside the land of Israel, readily adopted the Greek language and customs (in Israel, too, many Jews spoke and wrote Greek). The Septuagint, the Greek translation of the Jewish Scriptures, is thus a powerful expression of the extent to which the Jews in the late Second Temple period became Hellenized.

2) A second reason why the Septuagint is significant, particularly for our present study, is that it soon became the Scriptures of the early Christians. Already during the time of the apostle Paul, the early Jesus movement was spreading quickly throughout the Greek-speaking world (all of Paul's letters, like all the other writings of the New Testament, were originally written in Greek, not in Hebrew or Aramaic). For these early followers of Jesus, the Septuagint became their Bible. Whenever the authors of the New Testament quote from the Old Testament, as they frequently do, they quote from the Septuagint, that is, from the Greek translation of the Hebrew Scriptures, not from the Hebrew text of the Old Testament. Much of the vocabulary and even some of the religious concepts we find in the New Testament are based directly on the Septuagint. To this day, the Septuagint is the Old Testament of several churches, including the Roman Catholic and some Orthodox churches. In order for us to understand how the followers of Jesus interpreted Scripture, the Septuagint is indispensable.

3) Third, and finally, the Septuagint matters because it is different from the Hebrew Scriptures not just in language but also in content. In the previous chapter, we discussed the significance of the so-called Apocrypha, that is, the "extra" books that are included in the Septuagint. When the ancient Jewish scribes set out to translate their Jewish Scriptures into Greek, the collection of books they translated included some books that are not included in the Hebrew Jewish Bible. These books are known as the Apocrypha. Even in the case of the familiar biblical books such as Genesis and Jeremiah, the versions we find in the Septuagint differ from those in the Hebrew text, and at times the differences are significant. In other words, the book of Genesis in the Septuagint is not the same as the book of Genesis in the Hebrew text. Below, I will turn to the Septuagint and compare

its version of the biblical text with the Hebrew version of the Old Testament. The point of this comparison is to investigate exactly how the two versions differ from each other, and what these differences can tell us about early Jewish interpretations of the Bible.

1 Enoch

The scribes of the Second Temple period continued to write new books at an astonishing rate. While their books are new, typically the characters in them are not; they are familiar characters from Scripture. And it is very common to find that one of these biblical characters becomes the fictitious author of the book in which he appears.

It was a common practice among the ancient scribes of the Second Temple period not to write their own name when they composed a new book. Rather than telling us who they were and why they wrote, they preferred to write under a pseudonym. The most popular pseudonyms in early Judaism are the names of Old Testament characters. Scribes who lived a long time after the biblical period often chose a character from the Bible and attributed this newly written book to that character, as if it had been written in biblical times. In a sense, this is the opposite of plagiarism: rather than stealing ideas from a literary authority and writing them up under one's own name without properly documenting the source, here an otherwise unknown author writes a book and puts it into the mouth of an authoritative figure of the past. In scholarship, this rather common literary technique is called pseudepigraphy, from the Greek word *pseudepigraphos*, meaning "having a false title." It designates books that are falsely attributed to an author of the (biblical) past.

For a long time, modern scholars have had a hard time with this rather common literary practice of ancient Judaism (far from being particular to ancient Judaism, pseudepigraphy was also widely practiced among Christian and Latin writers). Scholars of the nineteenth and twentieth centuries thought that writing in the name of somebody else was simply wrong. In their understanding, the scribes were purposefully deceiving their readers by trying to pass their own books off as something that they were not. These books were forgeries, plain and simple, whose authors tried to hide behind their own texts and mislead their readers into thinking that these were inspired books written by the great authorities of the ancient past. It is only in recent years that scholars have begun to understand that to use modern sensibilities about what is or is not legitimate for authors to do and to hold ancient authors responsible to modern standards does not work. Rather than thinking of pseudepigraphy as an act of forgery, we should find some positive meaning in it.

Writing in the name of a biblical figure meant for the ancient scribes that they were continuing to write in the style of the Bible. In a sense, their books were intended to be sequels to the biblical books: the scribes chose a vocabulary with which readers of the Bible were already familiar, they used literary forms of expression their readers would have recognized from the Bible, and they continued to tell the biblical story, giving it some new and interesting twists. The choice of pseudonym signaled to the reader which tradition was being continued, that of the patriarch Abraham, for example, or of Moses the lawgiver, or of the prophet Jeremiah.

One of the most important books that was penned by Second Temple scribes is known today as 1 Enoch. It is attributed to a lesser-known figure from the Old Testament, the patriarch Enoch. Enoch makes only a very brief appearance in the book of Genesis. He is mentioned in Genesis 5:21–24 as the seventh in a list of ten patriarchs from Adam to Noah. It would be easy to miss him, were it not for a few peculiarities in his four-verse story that make him stand out. First, we notice that his lifespan is significantly shorter than that of all the other patriarchs in the same list. Enoch lived a total of 365 years, a number that immediately brings to mind the number of the days in the solar calendar. Second, the narrator says twice that Enoch "walked with God," which means that the patriarch was considered righteous and was especially close to God. And third, Enoch is one of the few individuals in the Old Testament who never dies. His life ended when God "took him." There is plenty of material in these four mysterious verses that invites interpretation and calls for fanciful expansions.

And this is precisely what happened after the book of Genesis was completed. Beginning in the third century BCE, the figure of Enoch became a popular pseudonym, and Jewish scribes began to write books in Enoch's name. The book we call 1 Enoch is itself a collection of several smaller books. In the middle of the twentieth century, one scholar famously proposed that 1 Enoch consists of five books and that these five books of Enoch were intended to be analogous to the five books of Moses in the Bible. Today it is clear, however, that 1 Enoch combines many more than five Enochic books, perhaps as many as fifteen. Enoch was a very popular character. Multiple copies of 1 Enoch were found among the Dead Sea Scrolls, and there is much evidence that the covenanters at Qumran greatly revered the book.

The most significant of the Enochic books for our purposes is the first of them, called the Book of the Watchers (1 Enoch 1–36). It tells the story of some heavenly angels, also known as the watchers (so called because they never sleep), who come down from heaven to have sex with human women. The story is told in a much-abbreviated form in Genesis 6:1–4. In the Book of the Watchers, the story is greatly expanded, and it is Enoch who is chosen to intercede on their behalf before God. After all, Enoch "walked with God," that is, he had access to the heavenly throne room. The story of the fallen angels enjoyed great popularity in early Judaism, and it is told in many different versions. We will return to it and discuss it below.

Jubilees

Some of the Second Temple scribes were the first translators of Scripture, and some composed new books. Others were the first biblical interpreters. When we think of biblical interpretation today, we tend to think of an interpreter who quotes a section from Scripture, a short passage, for example, or a verse, or even a single word, and then interprets it. This form of biblical interpretation was known already in ancient Judaism, to be sure, and we find examples of it in the Dead Sea Scrolls. But it is by no means the only way in which the Bible was interpreted by Jews in antiquity. In a different form of biblical interpretation, ancient commentators tried to blend the biblical text and their particular interpretation of it. This form of biblical interpretation took the form of rewriting, or rephrasing, the biblical text. Rather than quoting a particular passage and then commenting on it, the interpreter simply retold the entire biblical passage in the interpreter's own words, while leaving out certain parts of the biblical text, rearranging others, or adding new sections to it. To the modern reader this could seem problematic, like meddling with Scriptures, a reading *into* the biblical text rather than an interpretation *of* it. But in ancient Israel, this interpretive retelling of the Bible was a creative form of biblical interpretation. The point is not merely to highlight and clarify certain aspects in the text. Rather, in retelling the biblical story in one's own words, the biblical text becomes a vehicle for the interpreter to express some deeply held religious ideas and legal concerns.

A good example of this kind of biblical interpretation is Jubilees, a book written around the year 160 BCE. Jubilees is a retelling of the book of Genesis and half of the book of Exodus. It begins with the creation account in Genesis 1 and follows the biblical story line roughly up to Exodus 24, where the Israelites have wandered through the wilderness and arrived at Mount Sinai, and Moses has ascended the mountain to receive the law from God. The title of the book, Jubilees, stems from the fact that its author divides history into segments of forty-nine years. In Leviticus 25, the jubilee year is the fiftieth year in the calendar cycle. The calendar was a major concern for the author of Jubilees. The book asserts that the true calendar is not the lunar calendar as it is followed in Judaism today but the solar calendar of 364 days. This is the same solar calendar that was also followed by the members of the Qumran community and that underlies 1 Enoch.

Much like 1 Enoch, Jubilees was held in highest esteem by the members of the Qumran community. No fewer than fifteen copies of Jubilees were found among the Dead Sea Scrolls, a remarkable number that is a strong indication of its great popularity. In one of the foundational legal documents from Qumran, a text known as the Damascus Document, Jubilees is quoted in much the same way in which the author elsewhere quotes Scripture. This further suggests that Jubilees was revered as an authoritative text. The fragments of Jubilees that were found among the Dead Sea Scrolls are written in Hebrew, which indicates that the book itself was originally written in Hebrew. It was then translated into Greek and from Greek into other languages. The only complete version of the entire book of Jubilees that exists today is in Classical Ethiopic, or Ge'ez.

Jubilees is important for our purposes not because of how it interprets Genesis and Exodus but because of the religious concerns its author expresses. By rewriting Genesis and inserting significant new material into the biblical text, the author allows us to catch a glimpse of a particular kind of Jewish theology of the second century BCE, the date when Jubilees was written. In other words, what concerns us is not what we learn about Genesis by reading Jubilees. Our interest is in the author's religious concerns and original thinking, and how these thoughts are expressed through the vehicle of biblical interpretation. Of the recurring themes in Jubilees that define its theological stances—its concern for the 364-day solar calendar, and chiefly for the religious festivals; its preoccupation with matters of purity; and its insistence on the separation from Gentiles, to name but a few—particularly interesting is its description of the world of angels and demons. In the Torah, angels are only minor characters, they don't have names, and they are not developed very much as real characters in the plot. In Jubilees, by contrast, angels receive much more attention, and the author inserts them frequently into the biblical story. And Jubilees was not alone. From the second century BCE

46

onward, angels and spirits play a much more prominent role in many Jewish texts than they ever had before, including the New Testament. We will see several examples of this in the following chapters.

2 Baruch/4 Ezra

It remains difficult to determine exactly when many of the early Jewish books outside the Bible were written, especially when they do not mention any historical figures and do not refer to specific historical events. With regard to the last two books we will examine, known today as 2 Baruch and 4 Ezra, we are on much firmer ground. In the year 66 CE, the Jews in ancient Israel started a revolt against Rome, later known as the Great Jewish War. The uprising began in the north of the country but spread quickly. The Romans, who had little tolerance for such uprisings, were quick to suppress it: the Qumran community, which had nothing to do with the war, was destroyed in the year 68 CE; the Jerusalem temple was burned to the ground in the year 70 CE; and the last holdout by a small group of Jewish rebels, who continued to resist the Romans while encamped on top of a mountain plateau in the Judean desert called Masada, was defeated in 73 CE.

These two books, 2 Baruch and 4 Ezra, were written in the late first century CE, a generation or two after the fall of Jerusalem. Both are eloquent reflections on the catastrophic loss of the temple, its causes, and its consequences. How could God have allowed a gentile nation like the Romans to defeat God's people, to demolish the Jerusalem temple, and to erase all hopes and promises that were associated with God's protective presence in the temple? Was this an isolated event, or what else did God have in store for Israel? Where was Israel to go from here?

There is much 2 Baruch and 4 Ezra have in common. Both books were written in the late first century CE, most likely in Israel, possibly in or around Jerusalem. Both texts were originally written in Hebrew and were subsequently translated into other languages, although in neither case do we have any manuscripts with the original Hebrew text (both were written after Qumran was destroyed, so there are no copies of them among the Dead Sea Scrolls). There are several passages in which both books agree with each other word for word. That means that the two texts are clearly related to each other, but scholars have not been able to explain exactly how. And, as is true for 1 Enoch, both 2 Baruch and 4 Ezra are attributed to ancient figures of the Bible—in this case to Baruch and Ezra—even though the books that are named after them were actually written centuries after Baruch and Ezra lived. In the Old Testament, Baruch and Ezra are both scribes. Baruch was the personal confidant and scribe of the prophet Jeremiah (see, for example, Jeremiah 36), and Ezra was a priest and a scribe who returned with the exiles from Babylon and who publicly read and interpreted the Torah for all of Israel (see, for example, Nehemiah 8). The fact that Baruch and Ezra are both associated with the first destruction of the Jerusalem temple made them attractive pseudonyms for texts that were written in response to the second destruction of the temple. Several other books are attributed to Baruch and Ezra, hence the names 2 Baruch (to distinguish it from 1 Baruch, or simply Baruch, which is part of the Apocrypha in the Septuagint) and 4 Ezra (there are several books that bear Ezra's name).

These two sister apocalypses are important to us because they were written at the time of the New Testament. No other Jewish texts were written closer in time to the New Testament than 2 Baruch and 4 Ezra. Not surprisingly, we find significant thematic overlap between these two Jewish books and the books of the New Testament. 2 Baruch and 4 Ezra are both apocalypses, a new literary genre of the Second Temple period. The only way imaginable to repair the damage inflicted by the Roman destruction of Jerusalem was through divine intervention. Rather than dwelling on the past, both 2 Baruch and 4 Ezra imagine a future in which God defeats Israel's last enemy, restores Jerusalem, brings home those who are in exile, sends the messiah, resurrects the dead, and ushers in a new, incorruptible world. We will turn to them in greater detail in our discussion of the resurrection of the dead and the life among the angels.

A Time That Changed Israel Forever

The Old Testament was written over a period of roughly a millennium, from the twelfth to the second century BCE. It ended with the Second Temple period. German scholars of the nineteenth century called Judaism of the late Second Temple period *Spätjudentum*, or "late Judaism," a term they chose deliberately. It was intended to denigrate Judaism of the late biblical era and to portray it as a late, degenerate, and lifeless form of Judaism. In their opinion, by the time we get to the end of the Second Temple period, there is nothing left of the pure origins of the ancient Israelite religion, which these scholars saw most clearly embodied by the biblical prophets from the First Temple period. The term "late Judaism" was intended to leave no doubt that Israel had run its course and that whatever remained of it by the Second Temple period was soon to give way to Christianity, the *true* religion that infused the faithful again with a new spirituality. Soon Christianity would replace Judaism, a decrepit religion that had rendered itself obsolete.

This negative perception of the Second Temple period prevailed long into the twentieth century, even after its obvious anti-Jewish connotations had been recognized, and in some circles, it is alive and well today. The reasons for this negative view of Second Temple Judaism are complex. Lingering anti-Jewish sentiments, particularly among European Protestant theologians, certainly played a role, as did a general lack of knowledge about the late biblical period. The gap in the literary record of the Protestant Bible that largely glosses over four hundred years of ancient Jewish writings contributed to some misconceptions about Second Temple Judaism.

More recently, the perception of Second Temple Judaism has begun to change, and the significance of the changes that took place during this time is increasingly recognized. Historically speaking, the Second Temple period was the time when the diaspora became a permanent reality, when the first synagogues were founded, and when the new religious offices of the scribes and the rabbis emerged. Equally important were the changes that affected Israel's literature. A new class of highly trained scribes collected and copied the Jewish Scriptures, a process that would ultimately lead to the formation of the Bible. The last books of the Old Testament were written, several of them in the fourth century BCE and the book of Daniel in the second century BCE. The oldest biblical manuscripts date from this period. Scribes produced the first translation of the Jewish Scripture, the Septuagint. They interpreted Scripture and created new literary genres, such as the Tales of the Diaspora (Daniel 1–6; Esther) and the apocalypse (Daniel 7–12; 1 Enoch; 2 Baruch; 4 Ezra). And, most importantly for our purposes, Jewish authors of the late Second Temple period produced a wealth of new books and introduced a host of new topics into the religious debates—ideas that changed Israel forever. All of these ideas are picked up again and discussed extensively in the writings of the rabbis centuries later.

A century ago, scholars could not see the tremendous energy and innovative spirit of this remarkable period. They were quick to dismiss Second Temple Judaism as *Spätjudentum*, a late form of Judaism that, they argued, Jesus overcame. In the chapters that follow, I propose a dramatically different interpretation of the same period and of Jesus's place in it. Instead of writing off Second Temple Judaism as stagnant and obsolete, I will argue for its vibrancy and show its unique significance in the history of Judaism. And instead of posing Jesus in opposition to contemporary Judaism, I will argue that Jesus was deeply immersed in the Judaism of his time. When the texts of the New Testament are read in tandem with the Jewish books I have introduced in this chapter, the extent to which Jesus was an active participant in the religious debates of his time will become obvious. The Jewish world of Jesus is none other than the world of late Second Temple Judaism.

PART II

The Jewish Jesus

3

Jesus, the Messiah of Israel

The One Who Is to Come

The earliest followers of Jesus were united in their belief that Jesus of Nazareth, the son of Mary and Joseph, was the messiah for whom Israel had been waiting. Statements to this effect are found throughout the New Testament. In the opening scenes of the Gospel of John, for example, John tells the story of how Jesus meets his first disciples. One of them, Andrew, overhears John the Baptist bear witness about Jesus. He then looks for his brother Simon Peter and tells him excitedly, "We have found the Messiah." Then both Andrew and Peter go to follow Jesus. A short moment later the scene is repeated, albeit this time with a different couple of disciples. Now it is Philip who tells Nathanael, "We have found him about whom Moses in the law and also the prophets wrote, Jesus son of Joseph from Nazareth." When Nathanael meets Jesus shortly thereafter he says to him, "Rabbi, you are the Son of God! You are the King of Israel!" As early as the first chapter of his Gospel, John makes clear that it is a primary concern of his to demonstrate that

Jesus is the Messiah of Israel, in whom the messianic promises have been fulfilled.

A few chapters later, in John 4, Jesus is deep in conversation with a Samaritan woman. The two meet at Jacob's well in the city of Sychar and discuss the different places of worship of the Samaritans and the Jews. When Jesus tells the woman that soon all will worship God in spirit and truth, she responds with a reference to the Jewish hope for the messiah.

> [25] The woman said to him, "I know that the Messiah is coming" (who is called the Anointed). "When he comes, he will proclaim all things to us." [26] Jesus said to her, "I am he, the one who is speaking to you." (John 4:25–26; all translations from the Bible are taken from the New Revised Standard Version)

Andrew, Philip, and the Samaritan woman all speak of the Jewish belief in the coming of the messiah of Israel. Neither of them says very much about what exactly this belief entails, but a few things are clear: that the messiah will come to Israel, that the Advent of the messiah is thought to be imminent, that the Torah and the Prophets already announced the messiah, and that upon his arrival the messiah will reveal "all things." John also works an impressive number of messianic titles into the opening scene of his Gospel. At some point or another, those who hear of Jesus and meet him call Jesus "Lamb of God," "Son of God," "King of Israel," and "Son of Man"—all titles that are associated with the messiah and that are applied to Jesus in the first chapter of the Gospel of John.

Messianism, the belief in a divine agent whom God will send at the end of time to reign over a restored kingdom of Israel, was well established in first century Israel. The disciples of Jesus did not learn about the messiah from Jesus; they were already anticipating the coming of a messiah before they met Jesus. And they knew what to look out for. Likewise, the anonymous Samaritan woman, herself not an Israelite, also knew of the Jewish hope for a messiah who will come to reveal "all things." The belief in a messiah, a future anointed agent of God, is thus not a Christian innovation, as the New Testament makes abundantly clear. It did not originate with Jesus. Rather, traditions about the messiah are already attested in Judaism centuries earlier. Messianism has deep roots in the Old Testament, but the idea of an awaited agent of God only developed gradually in Judaism in post-Old Testament times, during the last centuries before the Common Era. The evangelists of the New Testament knew of these traditions and were deeply influenced by them. They portray Jesus of Nazareth in their Gospels as God's Messiah for whom Israel has been waiting, the One who is to come. Their aim is to show that Jesus of Nazareth *is* none other than the Messiah of Israel, who was already proclaimed in the Old Testament.

This chapter will trace the development of the messianic idea in ancient Judaism from its origins in the Old Testament to Jesus in the New Testament. The chapter begins with a selection of texts about the messiah in the Old Testament, then briefly examines some of the messianic expectations as they took shape in post–Old Testament Jewish writings, and finally compares these Jewish expectations with descriptions of Jesus in the New Testament. Not surprisingly, there are striking similarities between pre-Christian Jewish expectations of the messiah and the descriptions of Jesus we find in the Gospels.

The Messiahs of the Old Testament

The word "messiah" in English and its cognates in other Western languages come from the Greek word μεσσίας (pronounced *messías*). This explains why in English the word "messiah" is spelled with double "s." In the New Testament, which was originally written in Greek, the word μεσσίας is found twice, in the two places we have already discussed. In John 1:41, Andrew says to Simon Peter, "We have found the Messiah," and in John 4:25, the Samaritan woman says, "I know that the Messiah is coming." The Greek word μεσσίας is a loan word, meaning that it is not originally a Greek word but is adopted from another language. It is a Greek version of the Hebrew word *mashiakh* (in Aramaic, a language closely related to Hebrew, the word is meshikha). The Hebrew noun *mashiakh* derives from the verb *mashakh* (to smear; anoint) and thus means "the anointed one."

In addition to this Hebrew loan word, the Greek language has its own, native word for "anointed," χριστός (pronounced *christós*), from which comes the English word "Christ." It is related to the Greek verb *chrío* (to anoint). The words "Messiah" and "Christ" thus have the same meaning, "anointed one," only the former derives from the Hebrew and the latter from the Greek. The New Testament often refers to Jesus as "Jesus Christ," for example in the title of the Gospel of Mark in Mark 1:1, "The beginning of the good news of Jesus Christ." The Greek phrase "Jesus Christ" thus simply means "Jesus, the Messiah," or "Jesus, the Anointed." It is likely that for Mark and other authors of the New Testament, the word "Christ" meant more than simply its literal meaning, "anointed one." It had already become a messianic title.

The Hebrew noun *mashiakh* (anointed one) is found forty times in the Old Testament. There are three groups of people who are said to be "anointed": kings, priests, and prophets. The group most often called "anointed" in the Bible are the kings. Saul, Israel's first king, is called "the LORD's anointed," and so is King David, who reigned after Saul. Both carry this title because it was Samuel who anointed them and thus made them kings over Israel. In 1 Samuel 16, the Bible tells the story of how David is anointed as Israel's new king. When God sends Samuel to David's father Jesse to anoint the next king of Israel, Samuel has Jesse parade all of his sons before him. Only when David, the youngest of his brothers, is called to meet Samuel does God tell Samuel that this is the future king. This is when Samuel anoints David. "Then Samuel took the horn of oil, and anointed [Hebrew, *mashakh*] him in the presence of his brothers; and the Spirit of the LORD came mightily upon David from that day forward" (1 Samuel 16:13). This procedure of choosing the next king of Israel away from the public eye may seem a bit odd and somewhat underwhelming to the modern reader, who may well have expected a more impressive public coronation ceremony. And yet, in ancient Israel the act of anointing rather than public endorsement and celebration confers divine approval. The person is now set apart from the regular folk—and, in the case of David, against all odds endowed with the kind of authority that only God can bestow—regardless of how many people are present. The anointed individual now has a particular task with which God has entrusted him. The reasons for God's choice are rarely self-evident.

1) In addition to Saul and David, there are other kings who are also labeled "anointed" or "messiah" in the Bible. A curious example is King Cyrus the Great, the founder of the Persian Empire, not an Israelite, whom the prophet Isaiah calls "[the LORD's] anointed" (Isaiah 45:1). Cyrus was the Persian king who brought an end to the Babylonian captivity and allowed the Israelites to return home from exile. Calling Cyrus the LORD's "anointed" is Isaiah's way of saying that Cyrus, the only non-Israelite in the Old Testament who is called a "messiah," did what he did because it was the God of Israel who anointed him, endowed him with the authority to reign, and who saw to it that Cyrus would allow Israel to return home from exile.

2) The second group of individuals who are called "anointed" in the Old Testament are the priests. Chapter 4 of the book of Leviticus explains the nature of a particular kind of offering that was brought to the temple in Jerusalem, the offering for sins and severe personal impurities. The first case to be discussed in Leviticus 4 considers such incidents in which it is the high priest himself who sinned. The text begins, "If it is the anointed priest [a more literal translation of the Hebrew would be "the priest, the messiah"] who sins . . ." The Hebrew verb "to anoint" is used sixty-nine times in the Hebrew text of the Old Testament. Just about half of these cases relate to the anointing of Aaron and his sons, of the high priests, and of the various cult objects used at the temple in Jerusalem. It is therefore not surprising that the high priest in Leviticus 4 is said to be "anointed."

3) The third group, finally, are the prophets of Israel. Here the evidence is sparse. In 1 Kings 19, God tells Elijah to anoint two kings, Hazael of Aram and Jehu of Israel. God also commands

Elijah to anoint Elisha "as prophet in your place," but then the actual anointing of Elisha is never told. In Psalm 105:15, the psalmist recalls how God has always protected Israel since the time of Abraham, Isaac, and Jacob. The psalmist then notes how God rebuked the foreign kings, "Do not touch my anointed ones [or "my messiahs"]; do my prophets no harm." The phrases "my anointed ones" and "my prophets" are used in parallel lines in the psalm. In biblical poetry, two expressions that are used in parallelism typically refer to the same subject. The "anointed ones" in Psalm 105 thus are God's prophets. Apart from these short references in 1 Kings 19 and Psalm 105, there is no actual report in the Old Testament in which an individual is anointed to become a prophet. In brief, there are several people in the Bible who are said to be "anointed" —kings, priests, and, to a lesser extent, prophets. The act of anointing is part of their divine call and initiation rite. It bestows them with divine authority, even if they themselves do not become divine.

It is equally important to notice what we do *not* find in the Old Testament. While there are several individuals in the Bible who are said to be anointed, the word "messiah" or "anointed one" is never used in the Old Testament to designate a future anointed redeemer figure. In other words, there are no texts in the Old Testament that know of the concept of a messiah as an awaited agent of God, a descendant of David who will appear to reign over a restored kingdom of Israel at the end of time. That concept of a future messiah was only developed in later times, after the Old Testament. There are several "messiahs" in the Old Testament, to be sure, but they are *not* divine figures of the end of time. They are the kings, priests, and prophets of ancient Israel. And yet, when Andrew tells his brother Simon Peter, "We have found the Messiah," or when the Samaritan woman declares, "I know that the Messiah is coming," they are not referring to an earthly king, priest, or prophet. They are expressing the hope for a future redeemer figure, the messiah of the end time. We find that concept develop in the literature that was written during the gap years in between the Old and the New Testament.

The Scriptural Basis for the Messianic Expectations in Ancient Judaism

There are no texts in the Old Testament that speak of a future messianic figure of the end time. There are, however, several biblical texts that provide the scriptural basis for messianic expectations in ancient Judaism. A few of these biblical passages mention an "anointed" figure, but most of them do not. In Second Temple times, these texts came to be interpreted as predictions of a future messiah.

A recurring theme in the texts from the Old Testament that came to be interpreted as messianic prophecies is the hope that the messiah will be a royal figure who will come from the line of King David. This hope is grounded not only in the sheer majesty of King David, who is unparalleled among the monarchs in ancient Israel. It is also based on a particular promise of God to David. The book of 2 Samuel tells the gripping story of David's rise to power, tracing his rapid ascent step-by-step. First, David is made king over the entire kingdom of Israel. Then he conquers Jerusalem, a city that had not yet been taken by any of the tribes of Israel, and makes it the new political capital. Next, he brings the ark of the covenant to Jerusalem, so that the new political capital becomes the new religious capital as well. Then David builds himself a palace. And, finally, he offers to build God yet another structure, a temple that would serve as the new home for the ark. But this time David is rebutted. God sends Nathan to David to declare to him that the king should not build a house for God, but that it is God who will build a house for David. Nathan's oracle is a play on the word "house," which comes to mean both "temple" and "dynasty."

[11] Moreover the LORD declares to you that the LORD will make you a house. [12] When your days are fulfilled and you lie down with your ancestors, I will raise up your offspring after you, who

shall come forth from your body, and I will establish his kingdom. [13] He shall build a house for my name, and I will establish the throne of his kingdom forever. [14] I will be a father to him, and he shall be a son to me. When he commits iniquity, I will punish him with a rod such as mortals use, with blows inflicted by human beings. [15] But I will not take my steadfast love from him, as I took it from Saul, whom I put away from before you. [16] Your house and your kingdom shall be made sure forever before me; your throne shall be established forever. (2 Samuel 7:11–16)

Nathan's oracle does not focus on David's recent successes or on David himself, but instead looks to the future. God promises David an eternal dynasty, a Davidic kingdom that will exist forever. "Your house and your kingdom shall be made sure forever before me; your throne shall be established forever." Remarkably, the divine promise is an *unconditional promise*. The house of David will exist forever, regardless of whether Israel will follow the divine commandments. God will punish David's successor when necessary, to be sure, but the throne of David will never be in danger. Nathan uses familial language to express God's relationship with David's successor. "I will be a father to him, and he shall be a son to me." The monarch enjoys God's fatherly protection. God may discipline him, but he will never outright reject him. Later in the history of Israel, foreign empires such as the Babylonians and later the Romans conquered Jerusalem, and the throne of David *did* come to an end. But Israel never forgot Nathan's oracle and the unconditional promise that the house of David would exist forever.

The royal ideology in ancient Israel and the enormous hopes that centered on the king who occupied the throne of David are also expressed in the Psalms. One of these psalms is Psalm 2, one of the royal psalms in the Old Testament. Psalm 2 begins with a brief description of the situation that prompted its composition. A coalition of foreign nations has formed who conspire to rebel against Jerusalem. They are threatening to march against the city and defeat the king.

[1] Why do the nations conspire,
     and the peoples plot in vain?

60

> [2] The kings of the earth set themselves,
>   and the rulers take counsel together,
>   against the LORD and his anointed. (Psalm 2:1–2)

For the psalmist, the revolt by the foreign kings and rulers is not simply a revolt against the city of Jerusalem, it is a revolt against God and the king of Israel, God's chosen representative. The king, whose name is never given in the psalm, is here referred to as God's "anointed," or "his messiah." This use of the Hebrew term accords well with other places in the Old Testament where, as we have seen, the king is also said to be anointed. The psalm then goes on to relate how God merely laughs at the supposed threat by the hostile invaders. "I have set my king on Zion, my holy hill," God replies (Psalm 2:6). The implication is that God has chosen both the king and Zion, and no nation can undo what God has decreed.

Then the voice of the narrator changes abruptly from God to the king, who tells of his divine appointment and the promises he has received from God.

> [7] I will tell of the decree of the LORD:
>   He said to me, "You are my son;
>   today I have begotten you.
> [8] Ask of me, and I will make the nations your heritage,
>   and the ends of the earth your possession.
> [9] You shall break them with a rod of iron,
>   and dash them in pieces like a potter's vessel." (Psalm 2:7–9)

In these verses, the king remembers the moment when he assumed his royal office. While the king himself does not become divine, God calls him "my son." This is similar to our previous text, 2 Samuel 7, in which God promised David regarding his offspring: "I will be a father to him, and he shall be a son to me." The phrase in verse 7, "today I have begotten you," is commonly interpreted by scholars to reflect an enthronement ceremony of the new king in Jerusalem. The same language is used in similar ceremonies in other civilizations of the ancient Near East, particularly in Egypt. The king in Jerusalem remembers "the decree," that is, the royal protocol that was

61

presented to him at the time of his coronation. It was then that God declared that now the king had become God's "son." Since the monarch at this point is obviously an adult, the phrase "*today* I have begotten you" cannot refer to the moment of his conception. The language is clearly metaphorical. The ceremonial anointing of the king and his installation on the throne in Jerusalem are here expressed in adoption language. Through the act of anointing, God adopts the king as God's son. The father-son language in the context of the coronation is striking. The king has a special kinship with God and now is endowed to act as God's representative on earth.

In addition to 2 Samuel, which describes David's rise to power, and the royal psalms that declare the king in Jerusalem to be God's surrogate, a third group of texts served as the scriptural basis for the messianic expectations: the oracles of the biblical prophets. One particularly important prophetic text is Isaiah 11, an oracle that describes an ideal future king of the line of David. Isaiah 11 is closely related to Isaiah 9. Both passages praise the righteous reign of a future king of the Davidic dynasty, extolling the coming king in the highest terms. Like Nathan in 2 Samuel 7, Isaiah takes for granted that God has chosen the line of David forever. And just like the poet of Psalm 2, Isaiah believes that God has eternally chosen Jerusalem as the place of God's presence in Israel and as the seat of the king of David.

> [1] A shoot shall come out from the stump of Jesse,
>   and a branch shall grow out of his roots.
> [2] The spirit of the LORD shall rest on him,
>   the spirit of wisdom and understanding,
>   the spirit of counsel and might,
>   the spirit of knowledge and the fear of the LORD.
> [3] His delight shall be in the fear of the LORD.
> He shall not judge by what his eyes see,
>   or decide by what his ears hear;
> [4] but with righteousness he shall judge the poor,
>   and decide with equity for the meek of the earth;
> he shall strike the earth with the rod of his mouth,
>   and with the breath of his lips he shall kill the wicked.

⁵ Righteousness shall be the belt around his waist,
   and faithfulness the belt around his loins.
⁶ The wolf shall live with the lamb,
   the leopard shall lie down with the kid,
the calf and the lion and the fatling together,
   and a little child shall lead them.
⁷ The cow and the bear shall graze,
   their young shall lie down together;
   and the lion shall eat straw like the ox.
⁸ The nursing child shall play over the hole of the asp,
   and the weaned child shall put its hand on the adder's den.
⁹ They will not hurt or destroy
   on all my holy mountain;
   for the earth will be full of the knowledge of the LORD
   as the waters cover the sea. (Isaiah 11:1–9)

The text speaks of "a shoot" that will emerge from Jesse, David's father (1 Samuel 16). That shoot is a future royal savior, an ideal king of the Davidic dynasty who will sit on the throne in Jerusalem. The royal figure will be endowed with the spirit of the LORD. The prophet Isaiah lists in verse 2 three sets of gifts from the Spirit for the future glorious king: wisdom and understanding, counsel and might, and knowledge and the fear of the LORD. These are the attributes of the ideal king who is filled with the Spirit of God.

The second paragraph (verses 3–5) goes on to describe the reign of the Davidic ruler and his principal activity: he will act as a true and just judge. The dominant theme in this brief passage is righteousness. The king will judge with righteousness and show particular favor for the poor, the marginalized, and the meek of the world, while having no mercy on the wicked, whom he will kill "with the breath of his lips."

The third paragraph (verses 6–9) portrays an age of universal peace. The famous motifs of the wolf lying down with the lamb and the calf with the lion are well known from their many illustrations in the rich history of art. Isaiah's vision of the future harmony that includes all of creation is here closely tied to the rise of the righteous Davidic ruler. First, a new king is called from the line of David and endowed with the Spirit of

God. The king then executes the righteous will of God on earth, protects the meek, and defeats the wicked. And, finally, his righteous reign will lead to an unprecedented era of peace, in which all, humans and animals alike, can live together peacefully. The emphasis on the perfect Davidic king, the idealized view of the Jerusalem monarchy that will enable the entire world to enjoy equity and peace, provides an important clue about the occasion for which this text might have originally been composed. Scholars have proposed that Isaiah's oracle was originally part of a coronation ritual, most likely of a king who was crowned during the time of the prophet Isaiah. This king could have been King Hezekiah, but this has to remain a conjecture.

This famous description of the future king of the line of David who will rule over a kingdom of peace, in which "the wolf shall live with the lamb, the leopard shall lie down with the kid" seems so fantastic, so utopian, that it is not too difficult to imagine why early Jewish and Christian readers of the prophet Isaiah understood this passage to describe no ordinary king but the messiah, the anointed one of God, who will appear at the end of time to establish a messianic kingdom of peace, even though biblical scholars would argue that the text in Isaiah was likely composed for the coronation of a new king in ancient Israel.

A final text from the Old Testament we need to consider briefly that will play a prominent role in later messianic expectations is found in the book of Daniel. In chapter 7, Daniel, the book's protagonist, has a dream that troubles him greatly. In his vision, Daniel ascends into heaven, where he enters the divine throne room and witnesses a judgment scene. He sees God seated on the throne, with fire streaming from his presence and angels attending him all around. Then the last heathen emperor on earth, who is represented by a little horn that speaks arrogantly, is brought before God's throne. God condemns the emperor to death and destroys him. Next, Daniel witnesses a transfer of power. The dominion that used to belong to the emperor is now given to a new figure, whom the text merely identifies as "one like a human being."

> ^{13} As I watched in the night visions,
> I saw one like a human being
>   coming with the clouds of heaven.
> And he came to the Ancient One
>   and was presented before him.
> ^{14} To him was given dominion
>   and glory and kingship,
> that all peoples, nations, and languages
>   should serve him.
> His dominion is an everlasting dominion
>   that shall not pass away,
> and his kingship is one
>   that shall never be destroyed. (Daniel 7:13–14)

As soon as the emperor is condemned and put to death, Daniel sees "one like a human being" arrive on the clouds. The Aramaic expression, here rendered "one like a human being," can also be translated as "Son of Man." The figure is presented before the Ancient One, who is God. Then the "one like a human being" is entrusted with dominion over all the earth, which used to belong to the last emperor. He now rules victoriously, by God's appointment, and is king "in an everlasting dominion." The vision in Daniel 7 describes the transition from the last installment of history, a period of time represented by the horn that speaks arrogantly, to the transfer of power to the "one like a human being," who is installed by God and whose kingdom is eternal.

In the case of Daniel 7, we are better informed about the date of the passage. The story of Daniel's ascension into the heavenly throne room was written during a time when the Jews in Jerusalem were persecuted by the Syrian-Greek ruler Antiochus IV Epiphanes, who is the arrogant horn in Daniel's vision. The persecutions under Antiochus lasted for several years, from 167 to 164 BCE. Daniel's account of the judgment scene is intended to comfort those who suffer under the evil foreign emperor. Even though the Jews were still being persecuted when this text was written, according to this vision, the Greek tyrant had already been defeated in heaven, and his death had already been sealed, even if the Jews of Jerusalem could not enjoy their victory yet. But the promise of the vision is theirs.

Much has been written about the "one like a human being" who comes to God with the clouds of heaven. He is not a human being; he is "like" a human being, this much is clear. He is a heavenly figure who arrives on the clouds. Several proposals have been made regarding his identity. Given the book's interest in the heavenly realm, the "one like a human being" could be an angel—Gabriel, for example, or Michael, since both are mentioned by name in the book of Daniel. According to this interpretation, which is championed by many modern biblical interpreters, Daniel 7 describes a heavenly judgment scene in which God defeats Israel's last enemy and hands eternal rule over to one of his angels. But this is not the only way to read the passage. In the remainder of Daniel 7, an interpreting angel appears to Daniel and explains the vision to him. In the reading of the angelic interpreter, the "one like a human being" is not an individual at all but "the holy ones" (verse 22)—that is, the angels—and, a little later in the chapter, "the people of the holy ones of the Most High" (verse 27), that is, the people of Israel collectively. Accordingly, the promise of Daniel 7 is that while Israel is currently being persecuted, the eschatological moment when the tables are turned and God gives Israel full dominion over those who presently rule her is not far off. Finally, early Jewish and Christian readers of Daniel 7 had yet another interpretation. To them, there could be no doubt that the "one like a human being" was none other than the messiah of the end time, who arrives on the clouds and whose kingdom is an eternal messianic kingdom in which the messiah will rule forever. The biblical text is sufficiently ambiguous to allow for all of these interpretations.

These are some of the texts in the Old Testament that were interpreted as prophecies of a future messiah, even though this was most likely not their original meaning. Other biblical texts could be added, such as a collection of four poems in the book of Isaiah known as the Suffering Servant Songs (see Isaiah 42:1–4; 49:1–6; 50:4–11; 52:13–53:12). Here the poet describes an anonymous individual, chosen and sent by God, who suffers vicariously for the people. The Servant Songs, particularly the fourth one, are quoted often in the New Testament in descriptions of Jesus. All of these texts from the Old Testament were enormously influential in shaping ancient expectations of the messiah.

Messianic Expectations in Ancient Judaism

Expectations of a future "anointed" or "messianic" figure who will come at the end of time to restore the fortunes of Israel were widespread in ancient Judaism. A variety of extrabiblical texts include references to a messiah and to the messianic age. Before we turn to some of these texts, a brief word of caution is in order. While there are many pre-Christian Jewish texts that mention a messiah, we should not exaggerate their significance for ancient Jewish thought. The arrival of a messiah was expected to be part of the larger drama of the end time when many things will happen, among them the defeat of Israel's enemies, the return of Israel's exiles to Jerusalem, the resurrection of the dead, the last judgment, and the revelation of the New Jerusalem (the exact elements of the end time vary from text to text). The advent of the messiah is one of these events, but it is by no means the only, let alone the central, event. Moreover, the descriptions of the messiah and of his role vary significantly from text to text. In short, messianic expectations in early Judaism were widespread, but they were not of central importance, nor were they uniform.

The Dead Sea Scrolls are particularly significant in this regard, because they provide us with a glimpse of the diversity of Jewish messianic beliefs in ancient Judaism. Several scrolls express such messianic hopes. In what follows, we will look at two particular scrolls found at Qumran, the Messianic Apocalypse and the "Son of God" text. Both use messianic language.

We will compare these two texts from Qumran with the portraits of Jesus in the Gospel of Luke. The remarkable similarities that exist between the Qumran scrolls and Luke's description of Jesus suggest that even though it is impossible to prove that Luke knew these exact scrolls, he certainly was familiar with the kind of messianism that is expressed in them. For Luke, there is no doubt that Jesus is the messiah who is promised in these ancient Jewish texts.

The Messianic Apocalypse from Qumran

One of the scrolls that gives a vivid description of what will happen when the messiah comes is 4Q521 ("4" means that the text was found in Cave 4; "Q" stands for Qumran; and "521" is the number of the text). Modern scholars dubbed the text the Messianic Apocalypse, even though, strictly speaking, it is not an apocalypse but rather an end time prophecy in poetic form. This text, which is written in Hebrew, is known only from the Dead Sea Scrolls. It was discovered in the library at Qumran, although whether it was actually written at Qumran and therefore reflects the distinct theology of the Qumran community or whether it was brought to Qumran from another location is a matter of debate. The latter may be more plausible, since the text lacks any of the distinct vocabulary of the Qumran group.

The Messianic Apocalypse survives in a single copy, which, as is often the case with the Dead Sea Scrolls, is badly damaged. Scholars have reconstructed the text from no fewer than seventeen fragments. Most of these fragments are too small to be of any help, but a few passages are preserved well enough to be legible. The handwriting dates the scroll to the Hasmonean period, meaning that the Messianic Apocalypse was likely written during the first quarter of the first century BCE, roughly one hundred years before Jesus. The scribe wrote a few corrections into the text, which may suggest that the scroll that was discovered at Qumran is a copy of the text and not its original.

The following portion of the text is taken from fragment 2

(bracketed elipses such as [. . .] in the translation below represent missing or unintelligible passages in the text).

¹ [. . . for the heav]ens and the earth will listen to His messiah, ² [and all w]hich is in them shall not turn away from the commandments of the Holy Ones. ³ Strengthen yourselves, O you who seek the LORD, in His service! ⁴ Will you not find the LORD in this, all those who hope in their heart? ⁵ For the LORD seeks the pious and calls the righteous by name, ⁶ and His spirit hovers over the poor, and He renews the faithful with His strength. ⁷ For He will honor the pious upon the th[ro]ne of an eternal kingdom, ⁸ freeing prisoners, giving sight to the blind, straightening out the twis[ted.] ⁹ And for[ev]er shall I hold fast [to] those who [ho]pe, and in his mercy [. . .] ¹⁰ A man's rewa[rd for] good [wor]k[s] shall not be delayed. ¹¹ And the LORD will perform marvelous acts such as have not existed, just as He sa[id.] ¹² For he shall heal the badly wounded, He shall make the dead live, he will proclaim good news to the poor, ¹³ He shall sati[sfy] the [poo]r, He shall lead the uprooted, and the hungry He shall enrich (?). (Messianic Apocalypse; 4Q521 2 II, 1–13; my translation)

The first line of fragment 2 introduces the scene: heaven and earth will listen to "His" (presumably God's) messiah when the messiah comes. That means that the text takes the form of a prophecy of the end of time, a prediction of what will happen during the Advent of the messiah. The "Holy Ones" at the end of line 2 are not further identified, but we know from texts such as Daniel 7 and other Dead Sea Scrolls that they are most likely the heavenly angels, in this particular case possibly the heavenly entourage that will appear together with the messiah. Lines 1 and 2 thus claim that when the messiah comes, everybody in heaven and on earth will obey him and his angels.

In lines 3 and 4, the anonymous speaker turns to the audience and addresses them directly. They are called the faithful "who seek the LORD" and who "hope in their heart." The speaker calls on them to strengthen themselves, to be prepared and get ready for the time when the messiah arrives. This is a significant moment in the text, because it tells us something about why the text was written in the first place.

The Messianic Apocalypse does not simply provide a forecast of what will happen in the far-off future. It is an exhortation in which the speaker admonishes the audience to stay alert and to be ready. It also wants to give comfort to the faithful by telling them of the eschatological blessings that God will bring about and that await them.

Lines 5 and 6 are explicit about God's preferential treatment of certain groups: God will consider "the pious," "call the righteous by name," take care of the poor, and give strength to the faithful. The people who are being addressed in lines 3 and 4 by the speaker, those "who seek the LORD," will certainly have considered themselves part of the groups who are singled out in lines 5 and 6. As line 7 makes clear, God will sit "upon the throne of an eternal kingdom" (the text does not make clear whether it is God or the messiah who will sit on the throne, though the former seems more likely). In other words, this is not just another period in history, this is a description of a real change, the inauguration of a permanent, better reality that begins with the coming of the messiah.

Next the author provides a list of God's deeds at the time of the messiah, or, as line 11 of the Messianic Apocalypse calls them, the LORD's "marvelous acts such as have not existed." The list, which is rather specific, begins in line 8, is briefly interrupted in lines 9 through 11, and then continues in lines 12 and 13. In the preserved portions of the text, the list consists of seven blessings God will bestow: to free the prisoners, to give sight to the blind, to straighten the twisted, to heal the badly wounded, to resurrect the dead, to proclaim good news to the poor, and to feed the hungry.

Such lists of the events that will occur when the messiah comes are not uncommon in early Jewish writings. Another text, also from the first century BCE, is known as the Psalms of Solomon. It is a collection of eighteen psalms that are attributed to King Solomon, even though they were written at a much later time. No copies of the Psalms of Solomon were found at Qumran, so it is not one of the Dead Sea Scrolls. Instead, the Psalms of Solomon was composed in or around

Jerusalem in the immediate aftermath of the siege of Jerusalem in the year 63 BCE, when Pompey, the great Roman military commander, defeated the Hasmoneans, brought an end to their century-long rule, and conquered the holy city. The Psalms of Solomon was not written by the supporters of the Hasmoneans, and it certainly do not express approval for Pompey's invasion of Jerusalem. Rather, it comes from a third group that is identified in the text merely as "the devout." This group protests bitterly that the rule of the Hasmoneans and the invasion by the Romans were illegitimate, as both are unacceptable violations of God's will for Jerusalem.

Psalm 17 is most explicit in its lament over the current circumstances and in its appeal to God to send the messiah. The psalmist begins by recalling how, when God chose David to be king over Israel, God swore to David and to his descendants that the Davidic kingdom would never fall, an allusion to the promise in 2 Samuel 7 of an eternal Davidic dynasty. With Pompey's invasion of Jerusalem in 63 BCE, though, the psalmist is forced to admit that the kingdom *has* fallen. Now the psalmist turns to God, asks God to intervene, and specifically prays for the restoration of the Davidic monarchy.

[21] See, LORD, and raise up for them their king,
  the son of David, to rule over your servant Israel
  in the time known to you, O God.
[22] Gird him with the strength to destroy the unrighteous rulers,
  to purge Jerusalem from gentiles
  who trample her to destruction;
[23] in wisdom and in righteousness to drive out
  the sinners from the inheritance;
  to smash the arrogance of sinners like a potter's jar;
[24] to shatter all their substance with an iron rod;
  to destroy the unlawful nations with the word of his mouth;
[25] at his warning the nations will flee from his presence;
  and he will condemn sinners by the thoughts of their hearts.
  . . .
[32] And he [shall be] a righteous king, taught of God, over them.
  And there will be no unrighteousness in his days in their midst,

for all will be holy and their king [shall be] the LORD's Messiah."
(Psalms of Solomon 17:21–25, 32; trans. R. B. Wright)

The psalmist is explicit about the situation that prompted the composition of the psalm. Jerusalem is currently governed by "unrighteous rulers" who "trample her to destruction," an unambiguous reference to the Roman invasion of the city. The foreign offensive compels the psalmist to call on God to raise up a righteous king for Israel from the line of David. Verse 32 makes clear that this king is none other than "the LORD's Messiah." This Davidic messiah, for whom the psalmist prays, is a royal messiah. He is a military ruler who rules with force, defeats Israel's enemies, cleanses the city of its Gentile occupation, and destroys "the unlawful nations." This form of messianic expectation, which does not shy away from using language of violence to describe the activities of the messiah, is borne out of a specific historical situation: the violence that had previously been committed against Jerusalem. Some of the motifs that describe the activities of the messiah are biblical allusions. Among the biblical texts that underlie the psalm is Isaiah 11, the description of the future king of the line of David. The messiah in Psalms of Solomon 17 will be endowed with wisdom and strength (Isaiah 11:2), and he will destroy the unlawful "with the word of his mouth" (Isaiah 11:4). Another scriptural proof text from the Old Testament is Psalm 2, whose king will be victorious over the rulers of the nations.

But we need to return to the Messianic Apocalypse. How can the author of this text from Qumran be so certain about God's eschatological blessings in the messianic age? Where does this catalogue of God's "marvelous acts such as have not existed" come from? Much like in the case of the Psalms of Solomon, the description of God's deeds is heavily dependent on the Old Testament, particularly on the biblical psalms and on the prophet Isaiah. One of the key texts that underlies the Messianic Apocalypse is Psalm 146, a biblical hymn in praise of God the Creator and Redeemer. The psalmist lists several of the divine attributes, characteristics of the God of Israel that are so marvelous that they simply demand Israel's praise. This list overlaps partially with the list of the divine blessings in the Messianic Apocalypse.

> [7] [It is the LORD] who executes justice for the oppressed;
>   who gives food to the hungry.
> The LORD sets the prisoners free;
>   [8] the LORD opens the eyes of the blind.
> The LORD straightens out the twisted [or: lifts up those who are
> bowed down];
>   the LORD loves the righteous. (Psalm 146:7–8)

For the author of the Messianic Apocalypse, Psalm 146 is a prophetic text that predicts what God will do when the messiah comes to earth. There are four blessings that are shared by both Psalm 146 and the Messianic Apocalypse (even though they appear in a slightly different order): God feeds the hungry, God sets the prisoner free, God gives sight to the blind, and God straightens out the twisted. The psalmist's assertion that God "loves the righteous" (Psalm 146:8) is reminiscent of the assurance in the Messianic Apocalypse of the LORD's preferential treatment of the righteous, whom God will call by name.

In addition to Psalm 146, another biblical text figures prominently in the Messianic Apocalypse. This is a short passage from Isaiah 61. An anonymous speaker, who is not further identified in the text, relates in the first person how he has been called and set apart by God. God put God's Spirit on him, and God anointed him. We do not know who this person in the book of Isaiah is. It could be the prophet himself, since the first-person account resembles the prophet's call narrative (Isaiah 6), but this is not so clear in the biblical text. The passage in question reads as follows.

> [1] The spirit of the LORD God is upon me,
>   because the Lord has anointed me;
> he has sent me to bring good news to the oppressed,
>   to bind up the brokenhearted,
> to proclaim liberty to the captives,
>   and release to the prisoners;
>   [2] to proclaim the year of the LORD's favor,

and the day of vengeance of our God;
to comfort all who mourn. (Isaiah 61:1–2)

The anonymous speaker in Isaiah 61 recalls how God has endowed him with the divine Spirit and has anointed him. Indeed, the Spirit is upon him "because" God has anointed him. The speaker then goes on to relate the specific tasks of his mission, with which God has entrusted him. These tasks are expressed in a string of infinitives: "[God] has sent me to bring good news . . . to bind up . . . to proclaim liberty . . . to proclaim. . . ." There is, once again, some overlap with the list of God's deeds in the Messianic Apocalypse: to bring good news to the oppressed and to release the prisoners.

Psalm 146 provided the author of the Messianic Apocalypse with a list of some of God's blessings, but the psalm never mentions a messiah. In fact, there is nothing in Psalm 146 to suggest that this is a text that talks about the end time, apart from the marvelous nature of the divine blessings. The situation is rather different in Isaiah 61. There, the anonymous speaker begins by recalling how God has sent the divine Spirit upon him. The Spirit motif recalls the anointing of King David, who was also endowed with the Spirit when Samuel anointed him (1 Samuel 16). It is also reminiscent of Isaiah 11, where the Spirit is mentioned repeatedly. What is more, God has "anointed" the anonymous speaker in Isaiah 61. It is easy to see how, for the author of the Messianic Apocalypse, the anointed figure in Isaiah 61 is none other than *the* anointed one, that is, the messiah of Israel who will come at the end of time. For the interpreter at Qumran, Isaiah 61 has become a biblical proof text that predicts the marvelous deeds that God will do at the Advent of the messiah.

Jesus, the Messiah of Israel

From Qumran, we jump into the New Testament. In Luke 4, we read of Jesus's travels to Galilee in northern Israel, after his temptation by the devil in the wilderness. Now Jesus returns to his home town, the city of Nazareth. It is the Sabbath, and Jesus goes to the synagogue, in Luke's words, "as was his custom."

[14] Then Jesus, filled with the power of the Spirit, returned to Galilee, and a report about him spread through all the surrounding country. [15] He began to teach in their synagogues and was praised by everyone.

[16] When he came to Nazareth, where he had been brought up, he went to the synagogue on the Sabbath day, as was his custom. He stood up to read, [17] and the scroll of the prophet Isaiah was given to him. He unrolled the scroll and found the place where it was written:

[18] "The Spirit of the LORD is upon me,
    because he has anointed me to bring good news to the poor.
He has sent me to proclaim release to the captives
    and recovery of sight to the blind, to let the oppressed go free,
[19] to proclaim the year of the LORD's favor."

[20] And he rolled up the scroll, gave it back to the attendant, and sat down. The eyes of all in the synagogue were fixed on him. [21] Then he began to say to them, "Today this scripture has been fulfilled in your hearing." [22] All spoke well of him and were amazed at the gracious words that came from his mouth. (Luke 4:14–22)

The story of Jesus in the synagogue in Nazareth marks the beginning of his public ministry. It matters to Luke to portray Jesus as a faithful Jew who was deeply immersed in the Judaism of his time. It also matters to him to mention Jesus's fame, which he does repeatedly. In this particular scene, Jesus goes to the synagogue on the Sabbath. He is handed the scroll of Isaiah, unrolls it, reads a short passage, and then returns the scroll to the synagogue attendant. The prophetic passage Jesus reads, it turns out, is a conflation of two passages, both taken from the prophet Isaiah: Isaiah 61:1–2 and Isaiah 58:6. Isaiah 61 is the same passage that underlies the Messianic Apocalypse from Qumran. Isaiah 58 is a divine oracle in which God describes the form of worship that God prefers over the ritual fasts. "Is not this the fast that I choose: to loose the bonds of injustice, to undo the thongs of the yoke, to let the oppressed go free, and to break every yoke?" (Isaiah 58:6). In his reading, Jesus combines these two passages from Isaiah into one reading.

Why does Luke have Jesus read these particular verses from Isaiah? For Luke, Jesus is the anointed figure of Isaiah 61, who is filled with the Spirit. Notice how in Luke 4:1 and in 4:14, Jesus is already said to be filled with the Spirit. Luke thus prepares his readers for his claim that Jesus is the messianic figure of Isaiah 61 even before he introduces the text of Isaiah 61. Jesus brings good news to Israel and proclaims liberty to the captives. That prophecy, "to let the oppressed go free," which is part of Jesus's reading and comes from Isaiah 58:6, not only harkens back to the prophet Isaiah, it resonates even more deeply with the exodus story. God liberated Israel from slavery in Egypt and let the oppressed—that is, Israel—go free. Luke thus carefully anchors the life and teaching of Jesus in the history of ancient Israel. Jesus's ministry is the fulfillment of the hopes expressed by the prophet Isaiah, of Israel's yearning for the good news, for healing and liberty. This yearning is deeply grounded in the exodus story and God's liberating intervention. All Jesus has to say is, "Today this scripture has been fulfilled in your hearing." Luke wants to tell his readers: Jesus is the anointed one on whom the Spirit rests, the prophetic Messiah God has sent to proclaim the liberation of Israel.

A few chapters later, Luke provides yet another list of the events that are associated with the presence of Jesus, the Messiah. John the Baptist has doubts about who Jesus is and sends two of his disciples to ask Jesus directly.

[20] When the men had come to [Jesus], they said, "John the Baptist has sent us to you to ask, 'Are you the one who is to come, or are we to wait for another?'" [21] Jesus had just then cured many people of diseases, plagues, and evil spirits, and had given sight to many who were blind. [22] And he answered them, "Go and tell John what you have seen and heard: the blind receive their sight, the lame walk, the lepers are cleansed, the deaf hear, the dead are raised, the poor have good news brought to them." (Luke 7:20–22)

With the list in verse 22, Jesus provides a brief summary of his messianic role and of the healing acts of his presence. It is intended to answer John's doubts and, at the same time, reaffirm Jesus's identity as the Messiah. Jesus's reply is remarkably similar to the list in the Messianic Apocalypse from Qumran. The first and last element in Jesus's response, "to give sight to the blind" and "to proclaim good news to the poor," are also found in the text from Qumran. And there is a third element shared by both texts, the raising of the dead. There is no resurrection language in Isaiah 61. The Messianic Apocalypse and the Gospel of Luke draw heavily on the prophecies found in the book of Isaiah in their respective descriptions of the messiah, and yet, they both go a step further and add to their set of messianic expectations the hope for the resurrection of the dead. Luke leaves no doubt that Jesus *is* the anointed of Isaiah. But he also makes clear that there is more. He adds the resurrection of the dead. That addition, we now know from the Messianic Apocalypse, was not Luke's invention, but had become a fixed part of the messianic expectations in early Judaism by the time Luke wrote his Gospel. By including it in Jesus's response, Luke not only draws on the prophet Isaiah, he responds to the expectations expressed in the Messianic Apocalypse and confirms that Jesus is the Messiah.

The "Son of God" Text from Qumran

The second text to be considered from the Dead Sea Scrolls was also discovered in cave 4, which of the eleven caves in and around Qumran contained the largest number of manuscripts. The text, 4Q246, is written in Aramaic and, like the Messianic Apocalypse, dates from the first century BCE. This brief composition is known among scholars by various names, including the Apocryphon of Daniel or the Aramaic Apocalypse, though mostly it is referred to as the "Son of God" text, because of the figure of the "Son of God" who is mentioned in column 2.

This heavily fragmented text, whose beginning and end are lost, is divided into two columns of nine lines each. Column 1 begins with a brief story. An unnamed individual falls before a throne. The individual then goes on to address the king directly and to calm him down, because the king is troubled by a vision he has had. This sort of scene is well known from the book of Daniel, where it is Daniel who appears before the throne of King Nebuchadnezzar to interpret the king's dreams for him (Daniel 2 and 4); hence, the title for this text from Qumran, the Apocryphon (or "hidden," in the sense of "lesser known text") of Daniel. The seer offers an interpretation that involves "oppression" and "great slaughter in the provinces," and it also mentions the king of Assyria and Egypt. This period will come to an end, the seer goes on to explain, with the rise of one who will rule over the earth and who will be called great.

This is where column 1 ends and column 2 begins.

> [1] He will be called Son of God, they will call him Son of the Most High. But like sparks [2] that you saw, so will be their kingdom. They will reign only a few years over [3] the land, and all will trample. People will trample people and nation on nation, [. . .] [4] until the people of God arise; then all will have rest from warfare. [5] His kingdom will be an everlasting kingdom, and all his ways truth. He will judge [6] the land justly, and all will make peace. Warfare will cease from the land, [7] and all the nations shall do homage to him. The great God will be his strength. [8] He will fight for him, giving nations into his hand and [9] cast them all down before him. God's rule will be an everlasting rule, and all the depths . . . (Son of God text; 4Q246 II, 1–9; my trans.)

This short passage is difficult to interpret, mostly because we do not know who the Son of God figure in line 1 is and whether the different events that are described in this passage are sequential or simultaneous. These two interpretive problems are related. One group of scholars has pointed out that the text reads like a historical account. We should therefore assume that this is an apocalypse about the events that will unfold, one after the other, at the end of time; hence the title, the Aramaic Apocalypse. These scholars claim that the evils of the end time are here reported in their chronological sequence. Since the appearance of the Son of God in line 1 of the second column is followed in lines 2–3 by a time of uproar, bloodshed, and strife, they conclude that this must be an evil figure. He is an oppressive and wicked ruler who calls himself "Son of God" and "Son of the Most High" (both titles appear in line 1), but is, in fact, an impostor. Various candidates have been proposed. The individual in question could be a certain Alexander Balas, a Syrian-Greek ruler of the second century BCE. His royal name was Alexander Theopator (or "Alexander who has a divine father"), which is close to, but not quite the same as, "Son of God" in the Qumran text. The individual could also be the antichrist, who falsely claims for himself the titles and powers of the messiah. The problem with this interpretation is that the antichrist is not mentioned in any other texts from Qumran and is only found in later Christian texts.

A second group of scholars have proposed a different and, in my opinion, more plausible interpretation of the passage. Their argument is that "Son of God" and "Son of the Most High" are both titles of the messiah, and that the figure behind these titles in our text is not an evil impostor but the messiah. The biblical origins of these two messianic titles, they point out, are Psalm 2, the royal psalm in which God says to the king, "You are my son," and Nathan's prophecy to the house of David in 2 Samuel 7, in which God says about David's royal offspring, "I will be a father to him, and he shall be a son to me" (the title "Son of the Most High" does not have a biblical origin). According to this interpretation, the calamities of lines 2–3 are simultaneous with the Advent of the messiah; they are happening at the time when the messiah will appear. There will be much social unrest and oppression. In line 4, God raises up his own people, the people of Israel, and gives them peace. The remainder of the text in lines 5–9 describes an everlasting messianic kingdom. The precise nature of the messianic figure remains elusive, but a few details are clear: he will act as judge of the earth (lines 5–6), all cities will pay him homage (line 7), and no hostile nation can overcome him (lines 8–9). Again, the similarities with Psalm 2 are striking. In the psalm, God merely laughs at the alliance of nations that intend to attack Jerusalem. The current heir to the Davidic dynasty, whom God has anointed, will be victorious over Israel's enemies.

One of the reasons why the second interpretation of the Son of God text, which argues that the "Son of God" and the "Son of the Most High" are the messiah, is more plausible than the first is that this passage has an astonishing parallel in the infancy narrative in the Gospel of Luke. After the angel Gabriel has appeared to the priest Zechariah in the temple to foretell the birth of John the Baptist, Gabriel is sent to Mary to announce the birth of Jesus.

> [26] In the sixth month the angel Gabriel was sent by God to a town in Galilee called Nazareth, [27] to a virgin engaged to a man whose name was Joseph, of the house of David. The virgin's name was Mary. [28] And he came to her and said, "Greetings, favored one! The LORD is with you." [29] But she was much perplexed by his words and pondered what sort of greeting this might be. [30] The angel said to her, "Do not be afraid, Mary, for you have found favor with God. [31] And now, you will conceive in your womb and bear a son, and you will name him Jesus. [32] He will be great, and will be called the Son of the Most High, and the LORD God will give to him the throne of his ancestor David. [33] He will reign over the house of Jacob forever, and of his kingdom there will be no end." [34] Mary said to the angel, "How can this be, since I am a virgin?" [35] The angel said to her, "The Holy Spirit will come upon you, and the power of the Most High will overshadow you; therefore the child to be born will be holy; he will be called Son of God." (Luke 1:26–35)

The similarities between the expectations of the messiah in the Son of God text from Qumran and Gabriel's brief characterization of Jesus in the famous annunciation scene in Luke 1 are remarkable. Four phrases in particular are closely aligned: "he will be great" (at the end of column 1 of the "Son of God" text and in Luke 1:32); "he will be called Son of God" (line 1 of column 2 and Luke 1:35); he will be called the Son of the Most High" (line 1 of column 2 and Luke 1:32); and his "kingdom will be an everlasting kingdom" (line 5 of column 2 and Luke 1:33). It is difficult to be certain what to make of these similarities. One Qumran scholar, John J. Collins, goes so far as to speculate that Luke is dependent in some way on this text from Qumran and may have known of it. Of course, we cannot be certain. What is clear, however, is that when Luke uses these messianic titles and puts them into the mouth of Gabriel, he knows that his audience would have made the connection between Gabriel's annunciation and the contemporary Jewish expectations of the coming messiah, as they are spelled out in the Son of God text. That connection would have been lost on the modern reader of the Gospel, but because of the text from Qumran, we now know that there is nothing arbitrary about Luke's choice of words and that his characterization of Jesus is carefully chosen to answer the Jewish messianic expectations of his time.

Jesus, the Messiah of Israel

Messianism, the expectation of a messiah, an anointed agent of God who will come at the end of time to reign victoriously, was widespread in early Judaism. The concept of a messiah is not a Christian innovation. It has deep roots in the Old Testament and was fully developed in Judaism during the late Second Temple period. The early Christians inherited the belief in a messiah from their Jewish ancestors. By the time of Jesus and his first followers, messianic expectations had fully formed, even though the specific expectations varied from group to group. Some groups, for example, were expecting a royal messiah of the line of David who would restore the house of David, defeat Israel's enemies, and reign supremely in an eternal messianic kingdom. Others were hoping for a prophetic messiah who would heal the sick, release the prisoners, and proclaim good news to the poor. Others, still, were longing for a priestly messiah, the heavenly high priest. We find expressions of all of these forms of messianism applied to Jesus throughout the New Testament.

Jesus and the early Jesus movement did not emerge from the Old Testament; they emerged from the Judaism of their time, that is, from Judaism at the turn of the Common Era. The recognition that Jesus emerged from contemporary Judaism and needs to be understood in that context has direct consequences for the way in which we read the New Testament. Luke's descriptions of Jesus in chapters 1 and 4, the texts we have discussed above, are a case in point.

Let's consider the following two, rather different modern ways of reading the Gospel of Luke.

1. Old Testament → New Testament
2. Old Testament → Qumran → New Testament

In the first case, all we consider are the Old and the New Testament. The assumption is that Luke did not know of the texts from Qumran or the messianic traditions they express, that all Luke had in front of him was the Old Testament, and that he interpreted the Old Testament as he saw fit. His interpretation of the prophet Isaiah is new, unparalleled, unexpected, and intended to surprise his readers. In the second case, we are mindful of the evidence from Qumran, and we assume that when Luke wrote his story of Jesus, he was aware of the exegetical traditions that are attested at Qumran. Once we allow for the possibility that Luke knew the scrolls or the messianic traditions expressed in them, then he would not have been the first who interpreted these passages in Isaiah as predictions of the messiah. The question is whether there is a difference between these two modern ways of understanding the Gospel of Luke. Does our interpretation of the Gospel have to change, now that we know of the Dead Sea Scrolls? Do the scrolls make a difference for our understanding of Luke's Christology (his portrayal of Jesus)? The answer, I submit, has to be yes.

If all we had were the Old and the New Testament and no other Jewish literature, the fact that Gabriel calls Jesus "the Son of the Most High" and "Son of God" would seem incidental. We might think that these epithets are allusions to Psalm 2 or to the promise to the house of David in 2 Samuel 7. But there would be no reason to assume that these are specific titles that have any particular significance beyond these references to the Old Testament. Similarly, Luke's choice of Isaiah 61 as the Old Testament passage Luke has Jesus read in the synagogue in Nazareth would seem somewhat arbitrary; surely there are many other passages in the book of Isaiah Luke could have chosen just as well. The point of Luke's story, some have argued, is to set Jesus apart from the Judaism of his time and to show how Jesus broke with the Jewish community by interpreting the Scriptures in an unexpected way. Jesus is here countercultural, it has been claimed, in the sense that Luke creates an opposition between Jesus and the Jewish culture of his time. By claiming that the prophecy of Isaiah 61 has come true "today," Jesus engages in a subversive Bible reading that is intended to confront the Jewish authorities and to challenge the Jewish conventions of his time. Jesus uses the Jewish Bible against his fellow Jews.

This modern interpretation of the Gospel of Luke, and by extension of the entire New Testament, is predicated on the traditional view that Jesus emerged straight out of the Old Testament. The Jewish context of the New Testament is the Old Testament, and nothing else. This understanding of Luke is deeply misleading and fails on several grounds. First, it overlooks the many elements in Luke's Gospel that demonstrate how deeply Jesus was immersed in the Judaism of his time, elements the Old Testament cannot explain. Jesus goes to the synagogue, an institution that does not exist in the Old Testament. He reads from the prophets. If Jesus's reading is part of worship (Luke does not say this explicitly), then this would have been the public recitation of the *Haftarah*, the reading from the prophets that accompanies the Torah reading in Jewish services every Sabbath morning to this day. No *Haftarah* reading is ever mentioned in the Old Testament. In other words, this interpretation treats Luke's Gospel without any regard for its historical context. It claims, at least implicitly, that Luke's only context is the Old Testament—which it obviously is not.

Second, thanks to the Dead Sea Scrolls and other early Jewish texts, we are now much better informed about Judaism at the time of Jesus. Because of the Messianic Apocalypse and the Son of God text from Qumran, we can say with certainty that there was nothing arbitrary about Luke's choice of messianic titles and proof texts from the Old Testament. "Son of the Most High" and "Son of God" were used as titles for the messiah already a hundred years prior to Jesus, as the Son of God text shows. And the Messianic Apocalypse leaves no doubt that early Jews regarded Isaiah 61 as a messianic text that describes the events as they will unfold at the advent of the messiah. The astonishing similarities between the two texts from Qumran and the Gospel of Luke cannot be accidental. There can be little doubt, then, that Luke was intimately familiar with these titles for the messiah and with the most important messianic proof-texts from the Old Testament, and that he used both deliberately in his Gospel to make the case that Jesus is the Jewish Messiah. This does not take away anything from the originality of the evangelist. Quite the contrary. It shows how well-informed Luke was and how carefully his message is calibrated to answer a specific set of messianic expectations in contemporary Judaism. Jesus's interpretation of the prophet is not a countercultural reading of Isaiah, as some would have it. It is, in fact, deeply cultural, in that Luke skillfully positions his own use of Isaiah within the broader history of interpretation of the same passage in contemporary Judaism. There is, in other words, a layer of intentionality in Luke's Gospel that we are bound to miss if we insist, erroneously, that the Old Testament is the only Jewish context of the New Testament.

Third, it is a common feature of ancient Jewish biblical interpretation that certain biblical texts came to be interpreted in certain ways. Once a given passage from the Bible came to be linked to a particular interpretation, text and interpretation often merged and became inseparable. Above we looked at a number of passages from the Old Testament that were interpreted as predictions of the messiah. The same texts then came to be read as messianic prophecies by different groups and in different contexts. The same holds true for Luke. We now know for certain that when Luke has Jesus read Isaiah 61 in the synagogue, he follows an established tradition of reading Isaiah 61 as a messianic text. Luke did not invent the interpretive link between Isaiah 61 and messianic expectations. That's the whole point of the story. By using Isaiah 61, Luke triggers certain expectations in his audience, and then he goes on and makes the point that Jesus is that anointed one. To claim that this was Luke's own countercultural reading not only misses the important point, now proven by the Dead Sea Scrolls, that other interpreters who wrote long before Luke already interpreted Isaiah 61 as a prophecy of the messiah. It also rests on a deep misunderstanding of how the text of the Old Testament was copied, interpreted, and handed down from generation to generation in Jewish antiquity. Texts were inextricably bound to their particular traditions of interpretation. Luke was well aware of the messianic reading of Isaiah 61 and skillfully employed it in his portrayal of Jesus, the Messiah of Israel.

When I ask my audiences to compare Judaism and Christianity today, typically they will highlight the divisions that exist between the two religions. And the first difference that is commonly brought up is the belief in Jesus: whereas Christians confess that Jesus of Nazareth, the son of Mary and Joseph, is the Messiah, Jews do not believe that the messianic promises expressed in the Old Testament have been fulfilled. It is undoubtedly true that Jews and Christians are divided by what unites them, the belief in a messiah. But it is equally true that Christians inherited the idea of a messiah from Second Temple Judaism. And it is also true that even the ways in which Jesus is described in the New Testament, as we have seen in the case of the Gospel of Luke, are deeply Jewish, much more so than we would recognize if all we read was the Old and New Testament. Perhaps the divisions between Jews and Christians are not as deep as they appear.

4

———

In a World of Demons and Unclean Spirits

Demons and Unclean Spirits: A Naïve Misunderstanding?

Jesus and his followers lived in a world, the world of ancient Judaism, that was densely populated with demons and unclean spirits. Demons were ubiquitous. And they were thought to be real, in the sense that they could dwell in humans and wreak mental as well as physical havoc. A variety of maladies are attributed to their workings. According to the evangelists, unclean spirits could cause the inability to speak, hear, or see; they could induce epilepsy-like symptoms; and they could lead humans to insanity and even to self-destruction. Demons were a constant threat. It is therefore no surprise to find that in the Gospels, exorcisms are a central part of Jesus's ministry. The book of Acts relates how the apostles continued to heal the sick and cure those who were tormented by unclean spirits. The ability to cast out demons was thus passed on from the risen

Christ to the apostles and the leaders of the early church. It became a staple of the early Jesus movement.

For today's progressive Christians, the fact that Jesus conversed with demons and spirits is a source of embarrassment. "That's what people thought back then" is the modern response of those for whom stories about demons and unclean spirits merely reflect a naïve misunderstanding of what actually are physical disabilities and mental illnesses. But there is more to these stories than a primitive, premodern misperception of human diseases. The belief in the existence of demons and unclean spirits is predicated on the assumption—offensive to many modern believers and nonbelievers alike, no doubt—that human beings are not the center of all things. Humans are part of a larger reality that consists of more than just themselves. It includes other powers and forces as well as spiritual beings, some of them friendly and others hostile. Initially, the hostile spirits reside outside of the human body, but in an instant they can take possession of it, live in it, and cause significant damage, not unlike a parasite, or cancer. The demon resides inside the human body and lives off of it—but it does not belong there, it remains a foreign intruder. That means that the demon can be expelled again, or exorcised. The possessed can be freed from the intruder spirit and can be cleansed again. This kind of cleansing does not mean for the possessed "to be reconciled with oneself" or "to be made whole again," as healing is often understood in modern times. The focus in the New Testament stories is never on the possessed person, who hardly ever plays much of a role in the exorcism accounts and who always remains anonymous. Rather, the focus is on the encounter of the demons with Jesus, their complete powerlessness, and their instantaneous surrender.

When Jesus casts out demons, the evangelists make clear that this act of exorcism manifests the superiority of the kingdom of God as it breaks into the present world order. To the Gospel writers, Jesus's exorcisms are not incidental acts of kindness or random stories of healing. What Jesus is confronting is nothing less than an opposing power of a different kind, a well-organized kingdom of demons and unclean spirits. This powerful realm is ruled by Beelzebub, "the ruler of the demons" (Luke 11:15), whom Jesus calls Satan. When Jesus drives out the demons, he takes on the enemy of humankind. The ruler of the demons proves powerless against Jesus and the kingdom of God. Once a person has been freed of the invader spirit and liberated from Satan's oppression, Satan is defeated, at least temporally, and the person is free once again to receive the blessings of the kingdom of God.

Early Jews and Christians never questioned the existence of demons and unclean spirits, they simply took their existence for granted. To them, there was nothing extraordinary about this, as spirits of various kinds were part of daily life. There are no texts in the Old or New Testament that explain the origin and nature of demons and unclean spirits or that elaborate on their physical appearance and organization. Useful as such information might be for the modern reader, we find none of it in the Bible. To understand who these demons are, where they come from, and what they represent, we therefore need to look beyond the canon and turn to the Jewish environment of the New Testament. There we find a wealth of information about demons, with elaborate descriptions about their origins, the damage they can cause, how they relate to God and the angels, their names, and how they can be warded off. The silence in the New Testament is not the result of ignorance on the part of its authors. Quite to the contrary. Early Christian writers lived in a world in which such knowledge was widespread, so there was simply no need for them to rehearse what they could have safely assumed their readers knew already. For us today the situation is, of course, entirely different. To us, there is nothing obvious about demons and unclean spirits. We know little about the world the Gospel writers took for granted. To appreciate what exactly is happening when Jesus meets the demons, what is at stake in their encounter, and why these stories are so significant, it is imperative that we turn to the books of the Jewish world of Jesus. We need to read the exorcism accounts in the New Testament within their proper literary and historical context, the world of late Second Temple Judaism. Without such a comparative reading, we are not only bound to miss much in these texts. We run the risk of seriously misinterpreting the Gospel stories by relying exclusively on our own fancies about demons and their mischievous workings. The danger is that we impose onto the text what we think demons are. Our interpretation becomes ahistorical and arbitrary, a reading *into* the text as opposed to a learning *from* the text. A more responsible interpretation of Jesus's exorcism accounts acknowledges their Jewish setting and reads them in their proper context.

Jesus Meets the Demons

Of the four Gospels in the New Testament, Mark takes a particular interest in demons and unclean spirits. Even though his is the shortest of the Gospels, Mark has no fewer than four exorcism accounts (1:21–28; 5:1–20; 7:24–30; 9:14–29). Mark repeatedly refers to the demons in the summaries of Jesus's activities (1:32–34, 39; 3:11–12, 22–30). Power over demons is also part of Jesus's commission to his disciples (3:15; 6:7, 13; 9:38–39; but see 9:28–29). Demons and unclean spirits play a central role in Mark's story of Jesus's ministry.

This impression is further reinforced when we consider that the first healing story in Mark is an exorcism of an unclean spirit. Mark begins his Gospel with John the Baptist and Jesus's baptism (1:2–11). This is followed by the brief temptation account of Jesus in the wilderness (1:12–15) and the call of the first disciples (1:16–20). Now Jesus and a small group of his followers move to Capernaum, a Jewish fishing town on the northwestern shore of the Sea of Galilee. This is where our story begins.

[21] They went to Capernaum; and when the Sabbath came, he entered the synagogue and taught. [22] They were astounded at his teaching, for he taught them as one having authority, and not as the scribes. [23] Just then there was in their synagogue a man with an unclean spirit, [24] and he cried out, "What have you to do with us, Jesus of Nazareth? Have you come to destroy us? I know

who you are, the Holy One of God." [25] But Jesus rebuked him, saying, "Be silent, and come out of him!" [26] And the unclean spirit, convulsing him and crying with a loud voice, came out of him. [27] They were all amazed, and they kept on asking one another, "What is this? A new teaching—with authority! He commands even the unclean spirits, and they obey him." [28] At once his fame began to spread throughout the surrounding region of Galilee. (Mark 1:21–28)

Mark is a master storyteller, as this carefully crafted story about the man with the unclean spirit makes clear. He begins his account by setting the scene: Jesus enters the synagogue in Capernaum on the Sabbath day to read from Scripture and to teach (1:21). We are told right at the beginning that those who hear Jesus are astounded at his authority (1:22). Then, without much of a transition ("Just then . . ." is one of Mark's favorite expressions), Jesus meets a man "with an unclean spirit" (1:23). The spirit, not the man, immediately recognizes Jesus and addresses him directly. It is obvious that the spirit is on the defensive and fears being destroyed (1:24). Jesus sternly admonishes him to be silent and to come out of the man (1:25). The spirit has no choice but to obey. He comes out without an argument or fight, all the while torturing the poor man (1:26). Mark concludes the story with a detailed description of the spectators' amazement (1:27–28). The bystanders were already "astounded" at Jesus's teaching at the beginning of the story (1:22). Their continuous amazement thus frames the passage. As a consequence of the incident in the synagogue, Jesus's fame begins to spread throughout Galilee. In the evening of the same day, after he has healed Simon's mother-in-law (1:29–31), Jesus continues to "cast out many demons" (1:34; repeated again in 1:39).

At first glance, this is a story about healing. Jesus begins his public ministry by curing a man of his unclean spirit. But, as is often the case with healing stories in the Gospels, a closer look suggests that the healing only provides the occasion for the evangelist to tell a different story altogether. Mark tells us nothing about the man who is possessed, about his name, origin, the nature of his ailment, whether he had asked Jesus for help, why he was in the synagogue in the first place, and what happened to him after he was healed. The man remains largely invisible because the story is not his. A couple of chapters later, Mark tells another healing story, which is also set on the Sabbath, of a man with a withered hand (3:1–6). There, too, we learn little about the anonymous man at the center of the story or about the healing itself. That story is really about the mounting conflict between Jesus and his Jewish opponents, who immediately plot as to "how to destroy him" (3:6). The healing merely provides a convenient occasion for the conflict to build. If the situation is similar in our story in Mark 1, what, then, is the real subject of the story of the man with the unclean spirit?

The story is first and foremost a story about Jesus's encounter with the demon, a clash of two realms of power. Throughout his Gospel, Mark uses the terms "unclean spirit" (in Greek *pneuma akatartos*; 1:23, 26, 27) and "demon" (Greek *daimon*; 1:32, 34, 39) interchangeably and does not seem to distinguish between the two. The "unclean spirit" and "demon" are one and the same for Mark. One detail in the description of the demon is noticeable. When the demon first speaks to Jesus, he refers to himself in the plural. "What have you to do with us, Jesus of Nazareth? Have you come to destroy us?" (1:24). And when a little later the bystanders in the synagogue comment on Jesus's authority, they, too, speak of "unclean spirits" in the plural (1:27). There are different possible explanations for the unexpected use of the plural. In Mark 5, the story of the Gerasene demoniac, the second exorcism account in the Gospel of Mark, Jesus asks the demon about his name, possibly an exorcism technique, since to know the name gives power over the other.

> Then Jesus asked him, "What is your name?" He replied, "My name is Legion; for we are many." (Mark 5:9)

The Greek word "legion," which is a Roman military term, is a Latin loanword, from *legio* (an army; a large body of troops).

The demon in Mark 5 is in effect saying that the man Jesus is about to heal is possessed not by one but by two thousand demons. Something similar could be implied in our story in Mark 1 as well: since demons rarely come alone, the man in the synagogue may also be possessed by many demons, not just by one. But there is another way to interpret the plural. I suggested earlier that Jesus's exorcisms depict a clash of two kingdoms, the kingdom of God and the kingdom of demons. When Mark has the demon respond to Jesus in the first person plural, Mark may want to tell his readers that what Jesus confronts in this particular exorcism is not merely an individual demon but the entire demonic world.

And yet, what makes the encounter between Jesus and the demon so extraordinary is not the demon. To Mark, the demon does not seem to be all that interesting, since he tells us little about him. The demon is quickly evicted, and we are told nothing about what happens to him afterward. The situation is a bit different in the story of the Gerasene demoniac. In one of the better-known scenes in the Gospel, the demons beg Jesus for permission to enter into a herd of pigs that are standing nearby. He grants them permission, and the pigs, possessed by the demons, all drown in the Sea of Galilee.

> [11] Now there on the hillside a great herd of swine was feeding; [12] and the unclean spirits begged him, "Send us into the swine; let us enter them." [13] So [Jesus] gave them permission. And the unclean spirits came out and entered the swine; and the herd, numbering about two thousand, rushed down the steep bank into the sea, and were drowned in the sea. (Mark 5:11–13)

In neither story are we told what happens to the demons after they have been exorcized. In Mark 1 the demon disappears without a trace, and in Mark 5 the two thousand swine are drowned in the sea, much like Pharaoh's army was drowned in the sea when God delivered Israel out of Egypt, but we are never told the fate of the demons. Jesus is victorious, but he does not destroy the demons.

The most remarkable aspect about the demon in Mark 1 is

that *he knows who Jesus is* as soon as he sees Jesus enter the synagogue. In fact, the demon is the first in the Gospel of Mark to recognize Jesus. He first calls him by his name, "Jesus of Nazareth." And then he addresses Jesus a second time, now using a messianic title, "I know who you are, the Holy One of God" (1:24; this should be compared with John 6:69, where Simon Peter also calls Jesus "the Holy One of God," which for Simon Peter clearly is a messianic title). Jesus is "the Holy One of God," because earlier in the same chapter, when Jesus is baptized, the Holy Spirit descends on Jesus like a dove (Mark 1:10). In our story, the unclean, or "unholy," spirit immediately recognizes Jesus, who is now filled with the Holy Spirit and who has become the Holy One of God.

While the bystanders are "astounded" (1:22) and "amazed" (1:27) at what they hear and see, they cannot fully comprehend who Jesus is, whereas the demon gets it right away. All of this happens at the very beginning of the Gospel, during Jesus's first public miracle. The last person in the Gospel of Mark to make a public confession is a Roman centurion, a Gentile who, having witnessed Jesus's death on the cross, exclaims in amazement, "Truly this man was God's Son!" (15:39). These two christological statements about Jesus, one by the demon at the very beginning of the Gospel and the other by the centurion at the end, form a frame around the Gospel. Neither the demon or the Roman centurion is a follower of Jesus, yet they are the first and the last to confess Jesus in public.

It matters greatly to Mark to underscore how defenseless the demon is. As soon as the demon sees Jesus enter the synagogue, he realizes that he is in peril and cries out, "Have you come to destroy us?" (1:24). This is not an encounter among equals. No argument ensues; there is no struggle and no opposition. All the demon can do is acknowledge who Jesus is—"I know who you are" (1:24)—and to surrender unconditionally. Jesus is rather short in his reply, "Be silent and come out of him!" (1:25)—a mere five words in the Greek text. There is no elaborate procedure, no incantation, no ritual. The exorcism is over before it begins. In the third exorcism account in the Gospel in Mark 7:24–30, the story about the Syrophoenician woman whose little daughter is possessed by an unclean spirit, Jesus even evicts the spirit from afar, without ever going to visit the sick child. There is no need for Jesus to go and confront the demon face to face; Jesus's word is sufficient. It is the faith of the woman and her insistence that Jesus help her daughter that wins her the day.

> [29] Then he said to her, "For saying that, you may go—the demon has left your daughter." [30] So she went home, found the child lying on the bed, and the demon gone. (Mark 7:29–30)

One final aspect about our story has long caught the attention of Mark's readers. When the demon blurts out who Jesus is (1:24), Jesus's response is unexpected. Rather than embracing this public confession, Jesus does not want his true identity to be revealed and instead commands the demon to keep silent. "Be silent, and come out of him!" (1:25). The sentiment is again repeated a few verses later. That same evening, when Jesus casts out many demons, "he would not permit the demons to speak, because they knew him" (1:34). Jesus admonishes those who know him to keep his identity concealed. This motif, which is especially prevalent in the Gospel of Mark, has long puzzled interpreters. Modern scholars, who refer to it as "the messianic secret," have offered multiple interpretations as to why Jesus admonishes the demons to be quiet. The most plausible explanation may be to understand "the messianic secret" as a rhetorical device, a literary technique used by Mark and intended for the reader of his Gospel. Mark tells his readers that they cannot fully grasp who Jesus is until they have read Jesus's story all the way to the end. Jesus's true identity cannot be grasped from his teaching "as one having authority" or from his acts of exorcism alone, as impressive as these may be. Jesus's identity is revealed in the cross, and only in the cross; to understand that, the reader will have to read Mark's story all the way to its conclusion.

Are There Demons in the Old Testament?

Mark tells us nothing about the origin of demons; they are simply there. His exorcism accounts only provide the barest minimum of information about them. Demons are disembodied, supernatural beings who can dwell in humans and animals, even though originally they do not belong there. They are unclean and malevolent, and they can cause significant harm. Most importantly for Mark, the demons recognize Jesus immediately and address him with a curious mixture of utmost respect and dread, fearing for their lives. They realize that they are powerless, with no means to defend themselves. But Mark says nothing about where the demons come from.

There are no texts in the Old Testament either that explain who these demons are. In fact, there are no demons in the Old Testament, at least not of the kind we find in the Gospels. There are evil spirits in the Old Testament, but they are different from the unclean spirits in Mark. 1 Samuel 16 tells the story of how David became king of Israel. When Samuel anointed him, "the Spirit of the LORD came mightily upon David from that day forward." As soon as David is anointed, God's Spirit takes possession of David and empowers him to rule as God's chosen charismatic leader. All of this happens while Saul, Israel's first king, is still king. The Bible is rather uncompromising about the shift of power. As soon as Samuel anoints David, David becomes the new, spirit-possessed king, whereas Saul is no longer qualified to serve as king. This means that the Spirit of the LORD has left Saul. What is more, an "evil spirit" has taken its place, which afflicts Saul. "Now the spirit of the LORD departed from Saul, and an evil spirit from the LORD tormented him." The exact symptoms caused by the "evil spirit" are not further described. All the text says is that David is brought to Saul's court because he is a fine musician. Whenever God's evil spirit troubles Saul, David plays music for the ailing king to make him feel better. The concept of an "evil spirit" that stems from God in order to torment King Saul may be troubling from a modern point of view. In the Bible, it expresses the notion that Saul is rejected by God and devoid of the Spirit that originally allowed him to rule. The Spirit of the LORD has been replaced by an "evil spirit." This "evil spirit" is not a spirit that opposes God like the unclean spirit in the Gospel of Mark. It is, rather, a spirit that is sent by God to agonize the depraved king.

A similar story about a malevolent spirit is found in 1 Kings 22, the story about the prophet Micaiah, son of Imlah. Ahab, king of Israel, is considering going to war with the Arameans in order to regain control over the city of Ramoth-Gilead east of the Jordan river. Before he launches his attack, he seeks a divine oracle and consults with no fewer than four hundred prophets. The prophets ensure him a favorable outcome. Pressed by his ally, King Jehoshaphat of Judah, whether there are any other prophets to consult, Ahab reluctantly mentions a certain Micaiah, son of Imlah, a prophet he dislikes because in the past Micaiah's prophecies have always been unfavorable. When Ahab asks Micaiah about the outcome of the ensuing battle, the prophet predicts that Ahab will lose his life in the battle. So how can it be, the monarch wants to know, that all the other four hundred prophets, whose prophecies are favorable, are wrong? Micaiah answers with a story. He describes a vision of the heavenly throne room, in which he saw God sitting on the throne and the heavenly host standing beside God.

[20] And the LORD said, "Who will entice Ahab, so that he may go up and fall at Ramoth-Gilead?" Then one said one thing, and another said another, [21] until a spirit came forward and stood before the LORD, saying, "I will entice him." [22] "How?" the LORD asked him. He replied, "I will go out and be a lying spirit in the mouth of all his prophets." Then the LORD said, "You are to entice him, and you shall succeed; go out and do it." [23] So you see, the LORD has put a lying spirit in the mouth of all these your prophets; the LORD decreed disaster for you. (1 Kings 22:19–23)

The rather audacious story of Micaiah, son of Imlah, provides a fascinating glimpse into the inner world of prophecy in ancient Israel. The other prophets are wrong, Micaiah claims, not because they chose to tell King Ahab what he wants to hear but because God deliberately led them astray by sending them "a lying spirit" in order to send the king to his certain death. King Ahab chooses to ignore Micaiah's prophecy; he goes to battle, is mortally wounded, and dies, and Micaiah is vindicated. Like the spirit who tormented Saul, this lying spirit is sent by God. It does not oppose God, nor does it need to be exorcised.

If there are no "unclean spirits" in the Old Testament, are there any demons? The English word "demon" comes from Greek *daimon*, which means "god" or "attendant spirit" (the Latin word *daemon* also means "spirit"). That Greek term is attested in the Septuagint, the Greek translation of the Old Testament, but it has a different meaning in the Old Testament than in the New. One of the oldest texts in the Old Testament is Deuteronomy 32, a song that Moses sings for the assembly of Israel. In it Moses recalls how, when the Israelites wandered through the wilderness during the exodus from Egypt, they committed idolatry and worshipped foreign gods.

> [16] They made [God] jealous with strange gods,
>   with abhorrent things they provoked him.
> [17] They sacrificed to demons [Greek *daimon*], not God,
>   to deities they had never known,
>   to new ones recently arrived,
>   whom your ancestors had not feared.
> (Deuteronomy 32:16–17; see also Psalm 106:37)

In this passage, Moses is looking back at the exodus and recalling how the Israelites became unfaithful to their God and started to bring sacrifices to other gods. The word "demons" in verse 17 is referring to the gods of the nations—newcomers, as the psalmist derides them—whom the Israelites worshipped when they should have worshipped the God of Israel, whom their ancestors had revered for generations. These demons are also called "strange gods," for their main threat is that they lead the Israelites astray to commit idolatry. They are the gods of the nations that surrounded Israel at the time of the exodus, not the malevolent demons of the New Testament that possess individuals and cause grave bodily harm to the possessed.

Deuteronomy 32 uses the same word for "demon" that Mark uses as well, but the word has a completely different meaning in Deuteronomy. To conclude, the Old Testament does not know the demons of the New Testament, and it says nothing about their origin.

Where Do Demons Come From?

The story of the demons begins in the book of Genesis, even though no demons are ever mentioned in it. It begins with a brief and somewhat puzzling episode in Genesis 6:1–4, a short notice that relates how a group of heavenly beings abandoned their exalted status and came to earth to mate with human women.

> [1] When people began to multiply on the face of the ground, and daughters were born to them, [2] the sons of God saw that they were fair; and they took wives for themselves of all that they chose. [3] Then the LORD said, "My spirit shall not abide in mortals forever, for they are flesh; their days shall be one hundred twenty years." [4] The Nephilim were on the earth in those days—and also afterward—when the sons of God went in to the daughters of humans, who bore children to them. These were the heroes that were of old, warriors of renown. (Genesis 6:1–4)

This passage relates a strange incident that happened just when the human population began to grow on earth. The account is very terse and leaves much unanswered. This much is clear: A certain group of heavenly beings, who are called "the sons of God," a term that is generally taken to refer to the angels in heaven, saw that human women were beautiful, or "fair," as the text has it. The angels therefore decided to abandon their heavenly abode, come to earth, and have sexual relations with the women. These angels later came to be known as the "fallen angels," since they left heaven, effectively relinquished their angelic status, and subsequently found themselves unable to return to heaven.

In verse 3, the focus shifts from the fallen angels to human beings in general. It tells of God's decision to limit the human lifespan to 120 years (never mind that most characters in the book of Genesis lived significantly longer lives than that). What exactly the connection is between the episode about the fallen angels in verses 1–2 and the divine decree in verse 3 that humans may live no longer than 120 years is not made clear in the text. In verse 4, the story reverts to the angels again. A group called the Nephilim lived on earth at the time of the fallen angels. The Hebrew origin of the Nephilim is obscure, though it may be related to the Hebrew verb *naphal* (to fall). Most modern English translators simply leave the term untranslated. The Nephilim lived on earth at the time of the fallen angels. Verse 4 also states that the women bore children to the fallen angels. The passage ends with the brief note that these were heroes, "warriors of renown." Once again, it is not clear whether this remark refers to the Nephilim or to the offspring of the fallen angels, though the latter seems more likely.

Many questions remain about this short passage. One of the puzzles concerns verse 4 and the role of the Nephilim. What exactly is the connection between the Nephilim and the fallen angels, other than the coincidence that the Nephilim were around at the time when the angels came to earth? And what are we to do with the final remark about the heroic warriors? It is helpful to take a look at the Septuagint, because the Greek text of the same passage differs in some important aspects, particularly in verse 4.

> [4] Now the giants were on the earth in those days and afterward. When the sons of God used to go in to the daughters of humans, then they produced offspring for themselves. Those were the giants that were of old, humans of renown. (Genesis 6:4 LXX; my trans.)

What the Septuagint has preserved is not simply a straight Greek translation of the Hebrew text as we have it in our modern Bibles; it is a slightly different version of the story about the fallen angels. The Nephilim are gone and have been replaced by giants (the Greek has the word *gigantes*). In this telling of the story, the connection between the giants and the fallen angels is now clear: the giants in verse 4 are the offspring that stem from the illicit intercourse between the fallen angels and the women. The Greek text also says that the giants were around for a while, and that they were "renowned." In other words, the illicit liaison between the angels and the women *produced* the giants; their actions thus had far reaching consequences.

It is puzzling that the biblical author never condemns the angels for their actions. Neither in the Hebrew nor in the Greek version of the story are the rebellious angels ever criticized for what they did. Surely their behavior was less than noble, as they transgressed several lines at once: they came from heaven to earth, that is, they violated the boundaries of creation by abandoning the place that God had assigned to them; they did so merely because they were attracted by the looks of the earthly women, that is, their only motivation was their lust; and they went on to have sexual relations with the human women, who bore them giants, thus creating a new hybrid race. And still, there is no condemnation in the Bible of any of this. The only hint we get that the biblical author was less than approving of their actions comes from the context of the passage in Genesis. Immediately following the episode of the fallen angels, we read that human wickedness abounded on earth, and that things became so bad that God had second thoughts about having created humanity in the first place.

> [5] The LORD saw that the wickedness of humankind was great in the earth, and that every inclination of the thoughts of their hearts was only evil continually. [6] And the LORD was sorry that he had made humankind on the earth, and it grieved him to his heart. [7] So the LORD said, "I will blot out from the earth the human beings I have created—people together with animals and creeping things and birds of the air, for I am sorry that I have made them." (Genesis 6:5-7)

These are harsh words. The short passage mentions twice that God was "sorry" and "grieved . . . to his heart" to have created humankind, since the wickedness of humankind had become unbearable. The text remains silent about the origin of human wickedness, though given that the divine decision to undo the creation of humankind follows directly on the heels of the episode of the fallen angels, it may not be too far-fetched to assume that there is a connection. The sudden increase in human wickedness is linked to the angelic descent. The function of the fallen angel story in the Bible is to explain why the wickedness of humankind increased so exponentially that God felt compelled to undo God's own creation. The fallen angels are responsible for the deteriorating conditions on earth right before the flood, even if this is never spelled out in the Bible. God responded swiftly by sending the great flood, a punishment of monumental proportions.

In the book of Genesis, the story of the fallen angels is only a short episode. It is never picked up again anywhere else in the Old Testament. Given its terseness, the reader is left wondering: was this really all the biblical author knew about this unfortunate incident, or was there something so disturbing about the entire episode that the biblical author simply did not want to go into all the details but thought it best to record only the bare outline of the story? We may never know.

The Fallen Angels in Early Jewish Literature

Whatever the case may be, later Jewish writers did not have the same qualms. They were quick to pick up the story of the fallen angels and to develop it further, filling in many of the gaps in the biblical account. Beginning in the third century BCE, a number of Jewish authors told the story of the fallen angels anew, albeit in much greater detail. In what follows, we will look at three different texts, one from the third, one from the second, and one from the first century BCE. There is some evidence that these three texts build on each other, in the sense that the later authors were aware of the earlier texts and modified them to fit their own theological purposes. It is therefore of particular interest to observe not only how the story of the fallen angels changed over time but how, with each new rendition, the story acquired a new meaning.

In the expanded versions of the story, the fallen angels are called "spirits" or "watchers" (the term *watchers*, which is a direct translation of the Aramaic, implies that they do not sleep). The most elaborate version of the watcher story comes from a text that is aptly named after them, the Book of the Watchers. That book has come down to us as chapters 1–36 of 1 Enoch, a collection of several texts. The Book of the Watchers, which was written around the year 300 BCE, is devoted entirely to the fate of the watchers, their decision to come to earth, and their subsequent trial before God. It was written during a period in ancient Judaism that saw a remarkable increase in interest in the spiritual world. Early Jewish writers began to speculate about the spiritual realm and to write about spirits and demons at an unprecedented rate. In this remarkable literature, demonic beings are given names, and for some of them we are told specifically what they do. There is nothing comparable in the Bible. It is difficult to account for this sudden increase in interest in demons, though most scholars would probably agree that there may be more than one reason for it. On the one hand, early Jewish writers were deeply indebted to the Old Testament. They developed further what they found in the Bible. As we will see, the story of the fallen angels is one such example. And yet, on the other hand, we cannot exclude foreign influence. The literature of the ancient Near East, particularly the Babylonian texts, are filled with lesser deities, spirits, and demons, and there are some obvious connections between the Babylonian materials and the early Jewish texts.

The following passage from the Book of the Watchers is taken from the divine oracle that spells out the punishment that awaits the watchers. In this passage, God addresses the watchers directly.

15:6 But you originally existed as spirits, living forever, and not dying for all the generations of eternity; 7 therefore I did not make women among you. The spirits of heaven, in heaven is their dwelling; 8 but now the giants who were begotten by the spirits and flesh—they will call them evil spirits on the earth, for their dwelling will be on the earth. [9] The spirits that have gone forth from the body of their flesh are evil spirits, for from humans they came into being, and from the holy watchers was the origin of their creation. . . . [11] And the spirits of the giants lead astray, do violence, make desolate, and attack and wrestle and hurl upon the earth and cause illness. They eat nothing, but abstain from food and are thirsty and smite. [12] These spirits will rise up against the sons of men and against women, for they have come forth from them.

[16:1] From the day of the slaughter and destruction and death of the giants, from the soul of whose flesh the spirits are proceeding, they are making desolate without incurring judgment. Thus they will make desolate until the day of the consummation of the great judgment, when the great age will be consummated. It will be consummated all at once. (1 Enoch 15:6–16:1; trans. George W. E. Nickelsburg)

The opening paragraph of this passage makes clear that this is the same story as in Genesis 6:1–4. The text begins by providing a bit more information about the watchers before they came to earth, an aspect that is missing from the biblical version of the story. Originally the watchers were immortal spirits, or "spirits of heaven," as the text calls them, who lived forever. They did not have any women, because there was no need for them to procreate. God had decreed that the place of these spirits is in heaven, not on earth. The implication is that they should never have left their place of origin.

And yet, the disobedient spirits *did* come to earth and intermingled with human women, who then bore them giants. This reminds us of the Greek version of the story in the Septuagint, where we also read of the giants. The Book of the Watchers does not appear to have much interest in the giants themselves and thus tells us little about them, other than that when they died, evil spirits emerged from their bodies. The text is somewhat terse at this point, but elsewhere we are given a fuller version of the events. After the giants were born to the fallen angels, God decided to bring the deluge. This much is clear from Genesis 6. All of creation was drowned, including all of humankind (except for Noah and his family), all of the fallen angels, the women who bore them giants, and even the giants themselves. This should have been the end of the story, were it not for the fact that out of the deceased giants "evil spirits" emerged. The spirits are called "evil" because of their hybrid nature: they are the result of a transgression of the order of creation. And they are "spirits" because they are the offspring of the spirits who used to live in heaven. These spirits were begotten on earth, and therefore they are condemned to remain on earth, where they are known simply as "evil spirits." *These are the unclean spirits or demons that also appear in the New Testament.*

The passage in the Book of the Watchers then goes on to provide a fascinating catalogue of all the evils caused by these spirits. Many of them are also known from the New Testament. The spirits "lead astray, do violence, make desolate, and attack and wrestle and hurl upon the earth and cause illness." They are particularly aggressive against humans, presumably because they themselves are partly human. But their evil attacks will not go on forever, the divine oracle makes clear. The spirits will rage "until the day of the consummation of the great judgment, when the great age will be consummated." In other words, they will be active until the end of time. The Book of the Watchers is an apocalypse, and its author thinks in apocalyptic terms. The evil spirits emerged from the slain giants during the flood, and they will wreak havoc until the end of time. As long as this world lasts, there will be "evil spirits" who do violence and make desolate, but they will finally be vanquished at the consummation of the age.

The divine oracle from the Book of the Watchers provides some helpful context for our reading of Jesus's acts of exorcism in the Gospels. It tells the story of the origin of the demons: the demons emerged from the giants, who in turn are the hybrid offspring of the fallen angels and human women. It provides us with a list of their malevolent activities and explains why they afflict humans in particular: they themselves are partly human and are prone to turn against their own. And, most importantly, it illustrates why Jesus's unquestioned authority over the demons is so significant. According to the Book of the Watchers, the demons will be active until the end of time "without incurring judgment." And yet, Mark makes clear that Jesus has the power to stop and even to expel them *already now*. Demons are powerless before Jesus and cannot oppose him. Jesus does not destroy the demons, nor does he put an end to all of their mischievous doings once and for all. In this regard, Mark agrees with the Book of the Watchers that, in spite of Jesus's exorcisms, demons continue to be part of this world. But Jesus puts them in their place. He frees the possessed from their tyranny, cures the afflicted, and invites those who have been freed to receive once again the blessings of the kingdom of God. Jesus's acts of exorcism thus anticipate the total victory over all demons at the end of time, even though the final and complete destruction of the evil spirits still lies in the future.

The story of the demons was particularly popular in Judaism of the third and second century BCE. The next text is taken from Jubilees, a book written in the second century BCE—that is, a little over a hundred years after the Book of the Watchers and about two hundred years prior to the time of Jesus. Jubilees is an imaginative, at times fanciful, retelling of Genesis and parts of Exodus. While it follows the story line of the Bible in broad terms, it also introduces some new elements, short stories, and brief interpretive vignettes we won't find in the Bible, all intended to interpret the original biblical text. As will become clear, Jubilees is related to the Book of the Watchers. It is familiar with and uses some of the ancient motifs found in the Book of the Watchers, including the story of the fallen angels, but it gives them its own distinctive twist.

The following excerpt is set during the time of Noah and his offspring in the aftermath of the great flood. Like in the Book of the Watchers, the "evil spirits"—Jubilees calls them "demons" or "the polluted demons"—survived the flood and are now plaguing Noah, his children, and, in particular, his grandchildren. Jubilees relates how the children of Noah com-

plain to Noah about the activities of the demons and ask Noah
to turn to God and intercede on their behalf.

[1] In the third week of that jubilee the polluted demons began
to lead astray the children of Noah's sons and to lead them to
folly and to destroy them. [2] And the sons of Noah came to Noah,
their father, and they told him about the demons who were leading astray and blinding and killing his grandchildren. [3] And he
prayed before the LORD his God and he said: . . .

[4] "Bless me and my sons. And let us grow and increase and fill the
earth. [5] And you know that which the Watchers, the fathers of
these spirits, did in my days and also these spirits who are alive.
Shut them up and take them to the place of judgment. And do not
let them cause corruption among the sons of your servant, O my
God, because they are cruel and were created to destroy. [6] And
let them not rule over the spirits of the living because you alone
know their judgment, and do not let them have power over the
children of the righteous henceforth and forever."

[7] And the LORD our God spoke to us [the angels] so that we might
bind all of them. [8] And the chief of the spirits, Mastema, came
and he said: "O LORD, Creator, leave some of them before me, and
let them obey my voice. And let them do everything which I tell
them, because if some of them are not left for me, I will not be
able to exercise authority of my will among the children of men
because they are intended to corrupt and lead astray before my
judgment because the evil of the sons of men is great." [9] And he
said: "Let a tenth of them remain before him, but let nine parts
go down into the place of judgment." . . .

[13] And the evil spirits were restrained from following the sons of
Noah. (Jubilees 10:1–13; trans. O. S. Wintermute)

Just a couple of generations after the great flood subsided and
Noah's offspring were born, the demons began to assault them.
They led them astray "to folly" and even killed them. Devas-
tated by the loss of their children, the parents of the possessed
turn to Noah for help. Why to Noah? The Bible calls Noah
"a righteous man, blameless in his generation" who "walked
with God" (Genesis 6:9). The latter phrase, "walked with God,"

is particularly curious. It first appears in the Bible in Genesis 5:24, where it is used to describe a different figure, the patriarch Enoch, after whom 1 Enoch is named. Enoch never died because "God took him." Both Enoch and Noah have in common that God took a particular interest in them. They enjoyed the favor of God. Noah's children know all of this, and so they tell their father of the demonic devastations: the demons lead astray, they blind, and they even kill Noah's grandchildren. It is time for Noah to intervene.

Their plea does not fall on deaf ears, and Noah turns to God in prayer. Noah begins this section of his prayer with a petition, asking God for a blessing for his family, so that they can grow and fill the earth. Noah's opening petition is an allusion to Genesis 9:1 and 9:7, the covenant between God and Noah immediately following the flood. There, God blesses Noah and his family and commands them, "Be fruitful and multiply, and fill the earth." If God wants Noah's family to succeed, how can God allow the demons to kill Noah's offspring? Surely God does not want this. God needs no reminder of what the watchers, "the fathers of these spirits," did in Noah's days and what "these spirits" are doing today. Now Noah can make his appeal to God: he asks God to confine the demons and to bring them to judgment, so they can no longer harm his grandchildren. In other words, Noah asks God to limit their influence and to deprive them of any power they have over the living, and particularly over "the children of the righteous."

The divine response is swift to come. God commands his angels to bind the "evil spirits," presumably so that they can be handed over to be judged. In other words, God does what Noah has requested. But just as the divine decree is about to be executed, a certain Mastema appears before God and halts the action. Jubilees identifies him as "the chief of the spirits." Mastema, whose name in Hebrew means "adversary," is well known from other early Jewish writings, including the Dead Sea Scrolls. He is the chief leader of the demons, the equivalent of Satan. In this particular episode in Jubilees, Mastema pleads with God not to lock away *all* the demons, lest Mastema become completely powerless and no longer able to tyrannize the living. God heeds Mastema's plea, and a compromise is reached: nine-tenths of the "evil spirits" are thrown "into the place of judgment," a most dreadful place that is not further identified here, but of which the Book of the Watchers gives a vivid description, and God lets one-tenth of the spirits go free. These spirits are allowed to roam free, wreak havoc among humans, and continue to obey their master Mastema.

Jubilees tells the same story of the demons who emerged from the giants we have seen in Genesis 6 and the Book of the Watchers. But in Jubilees, the story is given a new purpose. It has become an etiology, a story of origins that seeks to explain a basic component of the human condition: it provides an explanation for the dark side of human life. It answers the question of why humans are afflicted by various ills and why they commit evil. This is all the doing of the evil spirits who act at the command of Mastema. Why did Noah not ask God for the total destruction of all demons, and why did God listen to Mastema? Jubilees uses the story about the origin of the demons to explain a reality of the human condition. There is no denying that illness and missteps are still part of human life today. So Jubilees had no choice but to allow some of the spirits to roam free—one-tenth, to be exact. And yet, Jubilees also offers some consolation. After all, God allowed only one-tenth of the demons to remain that initially afflicted Noah's grandchildren, the remnant of a power that has already been greatly curtailed. Things could be considerably worse.

Jubilees gives the story of the spirits yet another, theological twist. In this telling of the story, the demons are the cause of evil as it is experienced in daily life. While the demons do not come directly from God, their existence and their actions are nonetheless tolerated by God. After all, God listened to Mastema and granted at least part of his wish. Mastema himself, the leader of the demons, is subservient to God and can only do what God allows him to do. This is why he appears before God's throne in the first place and intervenes just as God is granting Noah's wish. Evil did not originate with God, but it is tolerated by God. According to the Book of the Watchers, the "evil spirits" will be around for as long as this world exists, but they will be defeated at the end of time. The same is true for the book of Jubilees. Mastema's days are numbered, and he knows it. This is the promise of Jubilees.

How to Ward Off Demons:
Advice from the Dead Sea Scrolls

Demons and evil spirits were a constant presence at Qumran. The rich trove of ancient manuscripts discovered in and around Qumran bears witness to a community that was deeply concerned about spirits and demons. According to the thinking of the Qumran group, human beings had free will, but at the same time they were subject to higher powers that ruled over them, including both angels and demons. The present age is under the dominion of the supreme demon, who is known by many names in the scrolls: Mastema (the same name that is used in Jubilees), Belial, Satan, and the Angel of Darkness. Copies of the Book of the Watchers and of Jubilees were found among the Dead Sea Scrolls, so there is clear evidence that the members of the community knew of these texts and revered them.

The people at Qumran were greatly concerned with protecting themselves against demonic powers. They cursed Mastema and his guilty lot in special ceremonies, and they recited incantations, prayers, and exorcisms to ward off his evil spirits. Among these texts are the Songs of the Sage. Written originally in Hebrew, Songs of the Sage are known only from the Dead Sea Scrolls, where they are attested in multiple manuscripts, a sign of their popularity at Qumran. It is estimated that the text was written in the first century BCE, that is, about one hundred years after the book of Jubilees. The text is attributed to the "sage" (in Hebrew, *maskil*), a member of the leadership group at Qumran who served as the head instructor. Speaking in the first person, the sage instructs his students and teaches them how to ward off demons and evil spirits.

^{1} [. . .] praises. Bless[ings to the K]ing of Glory.

Words of thanksgiving in psalms of ^{2} [splendor] to the God of
knowledge, the glory of the po[werful] ones, God of gods, LORD of
all the Holy Ones. [His] domini[on] ^{3} is over all the mighty strong
ones, and by the power of His streng[th] all will be dismayed and
scattered; they flee before the radiance of 4 His royal Glory. [. . .]

And I, the Sage, proclaim the splendor of his radiance in order to
frighten and te[rrify] ^{5} all the spirits of the destroying angels, the
bastard spirits, demons, Lilith, owls, and [jackals . . .] ^{6} and those
who fall upon men without warning to lead them astray from a
spirit of knowledge and to make their heart forlorn.

[. . .] desolate during the present dominion of ^{7} wickedness and
predetermined time of humiliation for the sons of lig[ht], by the
guilt of the ages of [those] defiled by iniquities–not for eternal
destruction ^{8} [bu]t for an era of humiliation for transgression.
[. . .]

Sing for joy, O righteous ones, for the wonderful God. ^{9} My psalms
are for the upright. [. . .] And [let] all those who are blameless
exalt Him! (4Q510 I, 1–9; also known as 4QSongs of the Sage; my
trans.)

The song begins with a title, "Blessings to the King of Glory." In
its original form, the song may have taken the form of a blessing of the God of Israel, a psalm of thanksgiving, as the first
line further clarifies. The first four lines of the song extol God,
praise God's unmatched qualities, and declare God's supreme
power. The language is intentionally dense and gives a taste
of how the original psalms would have sounded. God is the
"God of knowledge," the God who rules supreme over all other
gods, and the "LORD of all Holy Ones," most likely a reference
to the angels. So powerful and majestic is God that humans
and angels alike take flight. They are terrified, scatter, and flee
before his kingdom.

In the next three lines, lines 4–6, God's dominion is compared to yet another kingdom, that of the demons. The transition is clearly marked in the text by a change of speaker. In line

4, the sage inserts himself into the song and begins to speak in the first person. He is the song's main speaker, who proclaims the splendor of God's radiance. He does so, not simply to praise God, although that clearly is an important element in the psalm, but in order "to frighten and terrify" the dark powers. The recitation of the psalm is intended to ward off and neutralize the demons. In what follows, the sage provides a list of all the demonic powers: "the spirits of the destroying angels, the bastard spirits, demons, Lilith, owls, and [jackals . . .] and those who fall upon men without warning to lead them astray from a spirit of knowledge and to make their heart forlorn." This list of malevolent beings may not be a complete inventory of all the demons that are active in the world, neither does the list include a description of the sorts of harm they cause. But this was hardly necessary. The demonic powers are known from other texts at Qumran, which suggests that they were widely known and recognized.

Having named the dark forces one by one, the sage now turns to his hearers and addresses them directly. We may assume that these are his students, those to be instructed in the teachings of the community. The members of the Qumran community never identify themselves by name in their writings but prefer theological epithets. Here they are called "the sons of light," a self-designation that recurs elsewhere in the scrolls and that was also used by the early Christians in the New Testament (Ephesians 5:8; 1 Thessalonians 5:5). In the present age, the sage goes on to explain, God has placed them under the "present dominion of wickedness," and they are currently "humiliated." That is, they are subject to the demonic forces the sage has just enumerated for them. And yet, the end of this period of humiliation, which is synonymous with the end of this age, is near. That is the promise. It is not the members of the community who are destined for "eternal destruction" but rather "all the spirits of the destroying angels." In the final two lines of the passage, the sage calls on his hearers to rejoice in God. Here, he uses yet more epithets for his students. The "righteous ones," "the upright," and those "who

112

are blameless" are more designations for those who follow his instructions.

The Songs of the Sage relate how the sage teaches his students songs, blessings, and psalms of thanksgiving. The present age is ruled by wickedness. By reciting these songs and extolling the powers of God, the members of the Qumran community will be able to ward off demonic forces and protect themselves against their evil onslaught. Songs of praise and thanksgiving have here taken the place of curses against the demons. The current state of affairs will last until the end of this world, which is near. Then the evil spirits and demons are destined for everlasting destruction, whereas the faithful are promised an end to "the present dominion of wickedness."

All the Things Mark Took for Granted

When Mark begins his account of Jesus with the story about the man with an unclean spirit, he could have safely assumed that his audience knew who this unclean spirit was. Such knowledge was shared widely in ancient Judaism from the third century BCE onward, as the Book of the Watchers, Jubilees, and the Dead Sea Scrolls attest. Knowledge about spirits and demons had become a fixed part of the religious imagination by the first century CE when Mark wrote his Gospel. No one text provides a comprehensive and systematic account of the demons. Nor should we assume that all texts share the exact same concept of demons. They do not. But there was a basic set of beliefs regarding their origins and the nature of evil spirits and demons that was shared widely.

The demons are the offspring of the giants, those hybrid creatures who were born from the fallen angels and the women. They emerged when the giants were drowned in the flood. The demons survived the flood and continue to be the cause of various human afflictions, illnesses, sins, and other evils. They are well organized, some of them have names, and they are ruled by a leader, the chief of the demons, who is known by many names, including Mastema, the Angel of Darkness, Satan, or Beezlebub. Another thing on which all texts agree is that the demons cannot be destroyed. They are warded off, expelled, and bound, but never killed—at least not yet. Implied in these texts is an apocalyptic understanding of time: the demons remain alive and active in this world until the end of time, when they will finally be destroyed. This is made clear in the Book of the Watchers, Jubilees, and the Songs of the Sage.

Jesus's exorcism, too, is not yet a definitive manifestation of the kingdom of God. The kingdom is present in Jesus, to be sure; it has begun, but it is not yet fully realized. The significance of Jesus's acts of exorcism is that they prefigure and anticipate God's final victory over evil at the end of days, even if in the here and now that victory remains a promise. We still live in this world under "the dominion of wickedness," as the sage at Qumran puts it. And yet, in Jesus's encounter with the demons, the kingdom of God breaks into this world and proves victorious. This is the point of Mark's story, to provide assurance of the promise and to give a foretaste of how it will be—then, in a world without demons.

114

5

Did Jesus Abolish the Law of Moses?

Jesus and the Law of Moses

Did Jesus abolish the law of Moses? During my presentations on Jesus and the law in several churches, I was struck by two sentiments that I heard repeatedly from people in the audience. The first: At the time of Jesus, Jews had a rather narrow understanding of the law. Their religious lives were largely organized around the interpretation of, and strict obedience to, the law, which they took to an extreme. And the second sentiment: Jesus overcame this form of religion and freed his followers from the law. Jesus abolished the law and replaced it with love and common sense. He called on people to follow the Golden Rule and to love God and neighbor, which, after all, is much more sensible than following a primitive set of antiquated rules.

Why do so many Christians today believe that Jews at the time of Jesus were fixated on the law? One reason is the way in which the evangelists write about the debates between Jesus and the Pharisees in the Gospels. Far from being described in a neutral and objective manner, the Pharisees often come across as narrow-minded, hostile, and scheming. They are the "bad guys," the opponents of Jesus. In these short scenes in the Gospels, the Pharisees tend to serve as a foil against which Jesus's response seems like a breath of fresh air. From here it is only a small step for the modern reader of the New Testament to think that if this is what the Pharisees thought about the law, then truly all Jews must think the same. Another reason for the negative view is that all too often, stereotypical perceptions of rabbinic Judaism of a much later time, and particularly of the Rabbis' alleged understanding of Judaism as a religion of the law, are read back into the time of Jesus.

There are many problems with this sentiment. One is that the evangelists were simply not interested in giving us an objective description of the Pharisees. Their main objective was to show that Jesus is the Messiah of Israel. The actual Pharisees who lived in New Testament times were much more complex as a group and their views significantly more refined than what we learn about them in the New Testament. Another problem is that "the Pharisees" were not all of Judaism at the time of Jesus. They were only one of many groups, and each group had its own understanding of the law. It is therefore grossly misleading to draw any conclusions from Jesus's legal debates with the Pharisees, particularly as they are cast in the Gospels, about Jewish attitudes toward the law in general. Finally, we need to be careful not to project later forms of Judaism back into the time of Jesus. Quite apart from the fact that this is anachronistic, such projections are all the more problematic when the perception of Jewish attitudes toward the law that is being projected is itself pejorative and questionable.

With regard to the second sentiment, why is there such a pervasive sense among modern Christians that Jesus abolished the law of Moses? Here, too, multiple reasons can be given. One is the desire to set Jesus apart from his Jewish contemporaries, for example by drawing contrasts between Jesus and the Jews of his time. The argument runs something like this: whereas the Jews organized their religious lives around the commandments, Jesus freed his followers from the yoke of the law; whereas the Jews focused on following the letter of the law, Jesus cared about actual human beings and their needs; and whereas the Jews thought they could please God and become righteous through the works of the law, Jesus taught that the believer becomes righteous through faith by grace alone. Here, too, the pejorative descriptions of the scribes and Pharisees in the Gospels have played a significant role in giving rise to such stereotypes. Another reason why Christians maintain that Jesus abolished the law stems from the fact that Christians today do not follow the law. Since there are no religious obligations for Christians to circumcise their sons, abstain from work on the Sabbath, or keep certain dietary restrictions, it must be that Jesus already abolished the law. Christians today do what Jesus told them to do.

Once again, there are many problems with this sentiment. The most obvious problem is that this negative portrayal of Jewish attitudes toward the law is motivated by the desire to create an opposition between the negativity of the Jews and Jesus's positive interpretation. Such stereotyping is hardly based on an actual understanding of Judaism at the time, or at any time in Jewish history, for that matter. Another problem is the undifferentiated perception of "the Jews" and their supposed obsession with the law. "The Jews" simply becomes an abstract placeholder for "the other," that which is antiquated and which Jesus has overcome. Moreover, we simply cannot lump all groups together, and we certainly cannot assume that all groups shared the same understanding of the law, whatever that understanding might have been. A third and not so minor problem with this sentiment is that Jesus never says in the Gospels that he abolished the law. In fact, quite the opposite is true: in a famous passage in the Sermon on the Mount, a text in the Gospel of Matthew to which we will return later in this chapter, Jesus is adamant that he did *not*, in fact, abolish even a single letter of the law but instead came *to fulfill the law*. When we turn to Paul the apostle, who, like Jesus, had a lot to say about the law, we find that he held a similar position. Rather than abolishing the law, Paul, too, wants to retain it and recapture its original meaning.

This chapter consists of two main parts. In the first part, I will look at a variety of different understandings of the law in the Old Testament and in Second Temple Judaism, By examining different texts, we will see that Jewish conceptions of the law were far from uniform and constantly changed over time. Mosaic law was always held in highest esteem, but what exactly that meant differed from group to group. In the second part of the chapter, I turn to the New Testament and examine some of the most important passages on the law, focusing on Jesus and Paul. A close reading of the Gospel of Matthew and of Paul's letter to the Romans reveals, contrary to common sentiment, that neither Jesus nor Paul was intent on belittling, let alone abolishing, the law of Moses. Rather, both upheld it and recovered what they considered to be its original intention for their respective audiences.

The Origin and Meaning of the Word "Law"

The word "law" in the New Testament is a translation of the Greek word *nomos*. Greek *nomos*, in turn, translates the Hebrew word *torah* in almost all its occurrences in the Septuagint (the Greek translation of the Jewish Scriptures), and from the Septuagint it came into the New Testament. *Torah* is a noun that can mean "law," but it has a much broader range of meanings. Like most nouns in Hebrew, *torah* derives from a verb, in this case from the verb *yarah*, for which the dictionary provides several, rather different possible translations: "to point out; to show; to direct; to teach; to instruct." Accordingly, the noun *torah* can have multiple meanings as well. The dictionary gives three: "direction; instruction; law," though others could be added, such as "teaching." The English word "law" evokes certain legal connotations, having to do with rules of conduct that are enforced by an authority. In many texts, this is indeed what *torah* means, but it is important to bear in mind that the word itself means much more than that. To translate *torah* as "law" in every case can therefore be misleading, in that *torah* signifies much more than a set of specific legal proscriptions.

One of the basic meanings of the Hebrew word *torah* is "teaching" or "instruction." The book of Proverbs begins with a prologue that briefly summarizes the benefits of acquiring wisdom. The wisdom instructions then begin in Proverbs 1:8 with this proverb:

> Hear, my child, your father's instruction,
>   and do not reject your mother's teaching [in Hebrew, *torah*].

A similar sentiment is repeated again a few chapters later, in Proverbs 6:20:

> Keep, my child, your father's commandment,
>   and do not reject your mother's teaching [in Hebrew, *torah*].

The child, or student (the Hebrew word *ben*, literally "son," often means "student" in wisdom literature), who is being addressed here is admonished not to reject the parental instruction. In the first proverb in 1:8, *torah* stands in parallelism with "instruction," but the Hebrew word can also mean "admonition." And in the second proverb in 6:20, the equivalent word to *torah* is "commandment" (or Hebrew, *mizvah*). In both cases, it is the mother who provides the *torah* for the child, not the father. Clearly, here *torah* does not have a legal meaning but stands for wisdom instruction or general education. That education begins at home with the instructions from the parents.

Whereas in Proverbs, *torah* is understood more broadly as a form of parental instruction, in the book of Deuteronomy *torah* has an unambiguously legal meaning. In Deuteronomy 17, which is part of the Deuteronomic law (Deuteronomy 12–26), the word *torah* is used in such a legal context. The passage talks about cases of legal dispute that go beyond the authority of the local judges and hence need to be sent to the authorities at the high court, which is located at the central sanctuary. These authorities are the Levitical priests and the judges, and their decision is final. The text explains further:

> [10] Carry out exactly the decision that they announce to you from the place that the LORD will choose, diligently observing everything they instruct you. [11] You must carry out fully the law that they interpret for you or the ruling that they announce to you; do not turn aside from the decision that they announce to you, either to the right or to the left. (Deuteronomy 17:10–11)

Deuteronomy stipulates that the judges at the high court interpret "the law" (in Hebrew, *torah*) and then announce their ruling. The verb *yarah*, on which the noun *torah* is based, is used twice in this short passage, at the end of verse 10 ("everything they instruct you") and again at the beginning of verse 11 ("the law that they interpret for you"). Here, *torah* and the verb from which it derives, describe the judicial process, the legal decisions made by the highest authorities, the Levitical priests and the judges, who are specially appointed for this task.

Most commonly, however, the word *torah* designates the Torah of Moses, or what scholars call the Pentateuch, the first five books of the Bible: Genesis, Exodus, Leviticus, Numbers, and Deuteronomy. According to the tradition, the Torah comes from Moses. Thus, when Jesus quotes from the Torah in Mark 7:10, for example, he introduces the quote with "For Moses said." This tradition was then adopted by the early Christians (compare John 7:22; Romans 10:5).

The Torah in the Old Testament and Ancient Judaism

The following is a survey of four different texts, or text groups, from the Old Testament and ancient Judaism in which the Torah plays a central role. The survey explains how and when the word *torah* came to designate the Torah of Moses. It also illustrates how the word *torah* continued to have a rich variety of meanings and how different ancient groups and writers who wrote about the Torah had rather different ideas in mind. It is important for us to bear in mind that this plurality of meanings persisted well into the time of the New Testament and beyond.

Deuteronomy: Torah as the Torah of Moses

The book of Deuteronomy includes the first reference in the Old Testament to the Torah as a written document. Deuteronomy 17:14–20 explains the provision for the installment of a new king in Israel. As has often been observed, the so-called Law of the King in Deuteronomy 17, as this passage is known, is rather more intent on limiting the authority and prestige of the king than glorifying the king and his office. The law emphasizes the limitations of the royal office and says nothing about the king's actual powers. The only positive stipulation that the law mentions about the king is that he has to copy and study the Torah. "When [the king] has taken the throne of his kingdom, he shall have a copy of this law written for him in the presence of the Levitical priests" (Deuteronomy 17:18). Here "this law" (*torah*) clearly designates a book, God's instructions, of which the king is to produce a copy for himself, which he has to study constantly. Incidentally, it is this verse that gave the book its name, since "Deuteronomy" comes from the Greek *deuteronomion,* which means "a second, or repeated" (Greek, *deuteros*) "law" (Greek, *nomos*). The Greek entered into English via Latin (*Liber Deuteronomii*).

The word *torah* is used several times in Deuteronomy in the sense of "written document," or "law code" (see Deuteronomy 17:19; 28:58; 31:11–12). Deuteronomy also makes clear that it was Moses who wrote this particular document. Whereas according to ancient Jewish tradition, Moses was the author of all five books of the Torah, Deuteronomy is, in fact, the only book in the Bible that is explicitly ascribed to Moses. Nowhere does it say in the Bible that Moses wrote Genesis, Exodus, Leviticus, or Numbers; indeed, the Bible says nothing about who wrote these books. Things are different for Deuteronomy. In chapter 31, Moses makes arrangements for his death. First, he appoints Joshua as his successor. It will be Joshua's task to lead Israel into the promised land. Next, Moses turns his attention to his teachings and sees to it that they will not be forgotten. Whereas up to this point Moses has taught Israel only orally, he now decides to write his teachings down. This new document is called the Torah. "Then Moses wrote down this law (torah), and gave it to the priests, the sons of Levi" (Deuteronomy 31:9). Moses also arranges for the newly composed Torah to be read publicly every seventh year. Deuteronomy 31 does not say explicitly what it was that Moses wrote down, though it seems likely, based on the context, that "this law" in Deuteronomy 31:9 refers to the laws in Deuteronomy and possibly to other parts of Deuteronomy as well. Herein is found the origin of the tradition that Moses wrote all of the Torah, or the five books of Moses. Deuteronomy is, so to speak, the original "book of the Torah." Once Torah came to designate all five books of Moses, it was simply taken for granted by the ancient interpreters that Moses did, in fact, write the entire Pentateuch.

Following the death of Moses in Deuteronomy 34, Joshua becomes Israel's new leader. The next book in the Bible, aptly named after Joshua, tells the story of how the Israelites took possession of the promised land. Whereas in Deuteronomy, we find the first references to the Torah as a written document, it is in the book of Joshua that the Torah is first called "the book of the law (torah) of Moses." The first reference comes in Joshua 8:31, in which Joshua's actions are described as a fulfillment of Moses's explicit instructions, which he has left behind "in the book of the law of Moses" (the reference is repeated in Joshua 8:32). In the second reference, in Joshua 23:6, Joshua speaks to all of Israel in a large public address and solemnly admonishes them to remain steadfast and "do all that is written in the book of the Law of Moses." Both texts assume the existence of an authoritative document that goes back to Moses himself and that provides guidance for Israel. From now on, the Torah of Moses becomes a fixed term for a written document that is mentioned frequently in both the Old and the New Testament (see, for example, Luke 2:22; 24:44; John 7:23; and 1 Corinthians 9:9).

One other text in the Old Testament should be mentioned in this context. This is the story of the cult reform of King Josiah of Jerusalem in 2 Kings 22–23. Josiah ruled over Judah from 640–609 BCE. The story relates how, during renovation works on the temple in Jerusalem, a copy of "the book of the law" was found that prompted the king to start a major religious reform. Scholars commonly date Josiah's reform to the year 621 BCE. The story of the discovery of the book is told in 2 Kings 22.

> [8] The high priest Hilkiah said to Shaphan the secretary, "I have found the book of the law in the house of the LORD." When Hilkiah gave the book to Shaphan, he read it.... [10] Shaphan the secretary informed the king, "The priest Hilkiah has given me a book." Shaphan then read it aloud to the king. [11] When the king heard the words of the book of the law, he tore his clothes. (2 Kings 22:8–11)

Greatly disturbed by what he learns from the newly discovered "book of the law," King Josiah sends the priest Hilkiah and his associates to a certain prophetess named Huldah who lives in Jerusalem. Huldah, the wife of a temple official, then confirms that the content of the book does reflect the will of God. At this point, King Josiah starts a major religious reform that centers mainly on the removal of all traces of apostasy and idolatry from Jerusalem and Judah. This is the great cult reform of King Josiah.

The author of 2 Kings never tells us what is actually written in the mysterious book that was found in the Jerusalem temple; we can only extrapolate its content from the description of the reform it sets in motion. In his dissertation written two centuries ago, Wilhelm de Wette famously argued that Josiah's cult reform as described in 2 Kings 23 closely resembles the nucleus of the laws in Deuteronomy. He therefore concluded that the mysterious "book of the law" that Josiah found was none other than an early version of the book of Deuteronomy, a hypothesis that has since gained widespread acceptance. It is difficult to know whether the discovery of this early form of Deuteronomy in Jerusalem's temple actually happened, or whether this is a story invented by Josiah's supporters in order to lend divine authority and legitimacy to Josiah's cult reform. In either case, it is significant that the book of the Torah plays such a central role and that it prompts a major religious reform.

Ezra/Nehemiah: Torah as Israel's Statutory Law

From King Josiah, we jump to the Persian period and the time of the restoration in the fifth century BCE following the Babylonian exile. A significant shift in the perception of the Torah took place during the time of Ezra. While we see the very beginnings of legislative thinking in the book of Deuteronomy with "the book of the law" taking center stage, the idea of the Torah as *Israel's statutory law* is found only in the books of Ezra and Nehemiah.

Ezra returned to Jerusalem from Babylonia a little over half a century after the dedication of the Second Temple in 515 BCE. The biblical book that is named after him mentions repeatedly that Ezra was a priest (see Ezra 7:11, 12, 21; 10:10, 16). Ezra was also a scribe who was able to expound on the written word of the Torah, which he did with divine approval. Here is how the book of Ezra describes him:

> [6] [Ezra] was a scribe skilled in the law of Moses that the LORD the God of Israel had given; and the king granted him all that he asked, for the hand of the LORD his God was upon him. . . . [10] For Ezra had set his heart to study the law of the LORD, and to do it, and to teach the statutes and ordinances in Israel. (Ezra 7:6, 10)

The king who is mentioned in verse 6 is the Persian king. Presumably, Ezra needed the permission of the Persian authorities in order to give his law book any authority, since Judah continued to be under Persian control after the exile. The Persians were known for granting their subject nations a significant degree of freedom, so it comes as no surprise to see that the Persian king was happy to grant Ezra "all that he asked," possibly as a show of his benevolence. In any case, the biblical author is quick to point out that Ezra did not only have the approval of the Persian king, he also received the blessing from the God of Israel. Ezra had a divine mandate as well.

A pivotal scene is described in chapter 8 of the book of Nehemiah. The chapter offers a grand account of the first public reading of the Torah after the exiles had returned from Babylon to Jerusalem. The people gathered together in a large square, and Ezra stood on a wooden platform that had been built for the occasion. The scribe had been asked to bring "the book of the law of Moses" and to read from it to all who were assembled. After a brief ceremony at the beginning of the gathering, Ezra and his companions began their public reading. Every so often, they interrupted their reading in order to provide an explanation of what they had just read to make the text intelligible to the crowd. This went on for several hours:

> [5] And Ezra opened the book in the sight of all the people, for he was standing above all the people; and when he opened it, all the people stood up. [6] Then Ezra blessed the LORD, the great God, and all the people answered, "Amen, Amen," lifting up their hands. Then they bowed their heads and worshiped the LORD with their faces to the ground. . . . [8] So they read from the book, from the law of God, with interpretation. They gave the sense, so that the people understood the reading. (Nehemiah 8:5–8)

This celebratory reading of the Torah in Nehemiah 8 marks a crucial moment in the history of postexilic Israel. It points to the central role and function the Torah played for the returnees and for Israel as a whole. No longer merely a collection of some isolated biblical laws, the Torah became Israel's statutory law, the source of all legal rulings, and hence the very foundation of Jewish identity. From now on the Torah acquired a *prescriptive* function, in the sense that it came to define the Jewish way of life; it is the ultimate rulebook for what it means to be Jewish. The role of the Torah had changed forever, and so had that of Ezra the scribe. In the writings of the rabbis centuries later, Ezra is often compared to Moses: just as Moses gave Israel the Torah in the wilderness, so Ezra gave Israel the Torah after the return from exile. In this period of restoration, Ezra assumes the role of *a second Moses*, a new lawgiver. No longer a priest in the conventional, ritual sense, Ezra is the caretaker of the Torah, who reads publicly from it on certain occasions. He is also its chief interpreter, the one who derives from the Torah the divine teachings that become binding upon the courts and, indeed, upon all of Israel. In this regard, Ezra is the forebear of the scribes and textual interpreters of later centuries and, ultimately, of the Rabbis today.

Ben Sira: Torah as Wisdom

When we reconstruct the intellectual history of a concept or an idea, in this case the concept of the Torah becoming the authoritative rulebook in ancient Israel, it can be tempting for historians to reconstruct straight lines in the formation of the concept. The temptation is to identify certain moments in the past, line them up chronologically, and then claim that they represent progressive steps, one building on the other, in a linear development. We might be inclined to assume that these concepts developed in a linear way: first, Moses wrote down his teachings that were known as the Torah; then, the Torah became a book that was found in the temple and prompted Josiah's religious reform; and then, in Persian times, the Torah became the statutory law for all of Israel and Ezra its premier interpreter, much like the scribes and Rabbis after him. It would appear that there is a straight line here, an unbroken, direct, almost necessary development in the concept of the Torah. In reality, we know that things are never that easy and that the intellectual history of ancient Israel was much more complex. For example, the book of Deuteronomy was not written at the time of Moses but possibly during the Babylonian exile or even later, but most likely not that much earlier than the books of Ezra and Nehemiah. And with regard to Josiah's reform, we know even less about what actually happened.

While it is certainly true that the meaning of the Torah changed over time and that the books of Deuteronomy and Ezra mark important moments in that development, it is equally true that there were other groups in ancient Israel with their own understanding of the Torah. Their understandings, which were different from those described above, do not necessarily align neatly with this linear model. The literature of ancient Israel is as rich as it is precisely because there always coexisted multiple groups with multiple views on just about anything, particularly about the meaning of the Torah. This multiplicity of viewpoints increased during Second Temple times, with more groups emerging, writing their own texts, and developing their own world views.

One school of thought that is of particular interest in this regard and that has deep roots in the Old Testament is the wisdom tradition. The idea of divine wisdom played a major role in biblical Israel. Wisdom in the Bible means many things: it means a particular way of looking at the world and trying to detect a unifying, organizing principle behind everything; it means a way of life, a love for contemplation, learning, and instruction; and it means a certain kind of literature. In the Old Testament, there are several books scholars commonly count as wisdom literature: the book of Proverbs, for example, certain psalms, Job, Ecclesiastes (also known as Qoheleth), and Song of Songs. These books all share certain features. Whereas the Torah and the prophetic books are written for the most part in prose, wisdom books are written mostly in poetry. They include collections of proverbs that capture a certain truth. Whereas the Torah and the Prophets are largely concerned with the history of ancient Israel and its major events, wisdom literature tends to be remarkably void of any specific historical allusions. Its interest is in timeless truths, those aspects of life that are universal and not particular to ancient Israel. Wisdom books were popular not only in Israel but all over the ancient Near East, and there is much they have in common, even across cultural, historical, and linguistic borders.

Given that Israel's wisdom tradition is distinct from the rest of the books of the Bible in so many ways, it does not surprise to find that it has a different understanding of the word *torah*, too. We began this chapter with two verses from Proverbs, 1:8 and 6:20, both of which include the Torah. Here, torah is not a reference to Moses, and it has no legal connotations. Instead, Torah denotes parental instruction in general, the kind of teaching one can find in any house in which parents bring up and instruct their children. A look at other wisdom texts in the Old Testament confirms that Torah has a more general, nonlegal, and somewhat less specific meaning. Consider the following two examples, both from the biblical Psalter (that is, the book of Psalms).

> ^{1} Happy are those
>   who do not follow the advice of the wicked,
> or take the path that sinners tread,
>   or sit in the seat of scoffers;
> ^{2} but their delight is in the law of the LORD,
>   and on his law they meditate day and night. (Psalm 1:1–2)

> ^{1} Happy are those whose way is blameless,
>   who walk in the law of the LORD.
> . . .
> ^{18} Open my eyes, so that I may behold
>   wondrous things out of your law. (Psalm 119:1, 18)

Psalms 1 and 119 are frequently classified as wisdom psalms. In both of them, the Torah is at the center of the reflections. The author of Psalm 1 asserts that, unlike the wicked, sinners, and scoffers, the wise will meditate on the Torah "day and night" (see also Joshua 1:8). The call to always meditate on the Torah is reminiscent of the Law of the King in Deuteronomy 17 (indeed, there are several wisdom elements in Deuteronomy; the scribes who wrote the book were certainly well versed in Israel's wisdom tradition). Psalm 119, the longest psalm in the biblical Psalter, is called a "Torah Psalm" by modern scholars because its author frequently refers to the Torah. Both psalmists call on the reader to keep and meditate on the Torah, to teach the Torah, not to forget the Torah, to rejoice in it, and thereby to possess life. The Torah is spoken of in rather general terms as *a guide to life*. Any specific legal rulings are conspicuously absent. Indeed, both psalms remain deliberately vague about what exactly the Torah is, which can be frustrating for the reader who wishes to find more specific guidance. Psalms 1 and 119 attest to a kind of Torah piety, a certain lifestyle that involves meditation, reflection, and learning but that is not bound by a well-defined set of legal rulings.

The rich wisdom tradition in the Old Testament continued well into the Second Temple period. It found one of its most famous expressions during the Hellenistic period in the apocryphal book of Ben Sira (or Sirach), a wisdom book written in the second century BCE. Ben Sira, after whom the book is named, was a teacher and sage who had his own school, or "house of instruction" (Ben Sira 51:23), in Jerusalem, where he offered his classes. His book stands firmly in the wisdom tradition of the Old Testament. It consists of proverbs, the traditional literary format of the wisdom tradition, that are loosely collected according to their content, and that reflect on various aspects of life. Deeply rooted in the history and literature of ancient Israel, Ben Sira exhorts his readers to seek wisdom and fear the LORD.

Placed roughly in the middle of the book, chapter 24 includes a marvelous poem in praise of wisdom. Wisdom, here personified as a woman with divine attributes, speaks in the first person and sings her own praises. Lady Wisdom relates how, when she dwelled in heaven, she appeared in the heavenly council, where she spoke of her desire to come to earth. This heavenly scene is based on the motif of wisdom personified as a woman in Proverbs 8, the closest ancient Israel ever came to a female companion to the God of Israel. Wisdom relates in the first person how she traversed the earth in search of a home but could not find a place to stay, until God told her to live in Israel.

> Then the Creator of all things gave me a command,
> and my Creator chose the place for my tent.
> He said, "Make your dwelling in Jacob,

and in Israel receive your inheritance."
(Ben Sira 24:8; New Revised Standard Version)

Then Wisdom decided to live in Israel, in her words, among "an honored people." In what follows, she describes how she excelled after she had established her new residence, how her splendor far exceeded that of the tallest trees, and how she gave eternal sustenance. At this point, the narrator interrupts her hymn and interjects the following interpretive comment:

All this is the book of the covenant of the Most High God,
the law that Moses commanded us
as an inheritance for the congregations of Jacob. (Ben Sira 24:23)

The "book of the covenant" is a reference to the exodus story, when God entered into a covenantal relation with Israel. The Torah is the sign of that covenant. In the next line, Ben Sira qualifies "the law" further by adding the phrase, "the law that Moses commanded us." This makes clear that Ben Sira is thinking of the Torah of Moses, and specifically of that moment in the exodus story when Moses gave Israel the Torah at Mount Sinai. Wisdom is here linked to the Torah. Specifically, Ben Sira *identifies wisdom with Torah*. Ben Sira 24 is the first text in Jewish literature that explicitly identifies wisdom and the Mosaic Torah. In a brilliant move, Ben Sira inherits two originally distinct traditions, that of wisdom coming to earth (Proverbs 8) and that of the giving of the Torah at Mount Sinai (in the book of Exodus), and integrates them by identifying wisdom and Torah. For Ben Sira, wisdom is embodied in the Torah, as the Torah becomes wisdom. It is through the Torah that wisdom enlightens and leads the student to life.

A few centuries later, the first Christian writers will use the motif of wisdom coming to earth in their descriptions of Jesus. However, they will substitute Jesus of Nazareth for the Torah as the embodiment of wisdom. In 1 Corinthians 1, for example, Paul argues that Jesus is both the power of God "and the wisdom of God" (1 Corinthians 1:24). Similarly, in the prologue to the Gospel of John (John 1:1–18), it is the Word of God that was "in the beginning" and came to earth, much like wisdom in Ben Sira 24 was there in the beginning and later came to earth to dwell in Israel. For John, that Word is none other than Jesus. While Ben Sira identifies wisdom with Torah, Paul and John identify wisdom with Jesus.

The Dead Sea Scrolls: The Multiple Meanings of Torah

Unlike the texts we have looked at so far, the Dead Sea Scrolls are not a single composition but a collection of diverse texts, an entire library. Many of the scrolls were written at Qumran and therefore reflect the thinking of this particular group, but several of them originated elsewhere, and it just so happens that copies of them were found in the caves of Qumran. As a consequence, the Dead Sea Scrolls represent a broad spectrum of viewpoints, not just the opinion of the members of the community. The Torah figures prominently in many of these texts. All aspects of the Torah we have discussed above can also be found in the scrolls, as well as a few others.

For the Qumran community, the Mosaic Torah was, first and foremost, *the* central authoritative text and the source of all the rulings that defined their identity. The scrolls leave no doubt about the centrality of the Torah in the life of the community and repeatedly emphasize the importance of its correct interpretation. In one of the foundational documents, a text known as the Damascus Document, the author looks back to the origins and earliest history of the community. At a time when all of Israel went astray, God chose the members of the Qumran community and established a special, everlasting covenant exclusively with them. In this passage, the community is called "the remnant," an allusion to the motif of the obedient remnant in the prophet Isaiah. This marked the beginning of the community.

> But with the remnant which held fast to the commandments of God he made his covenant with Israel forever, revealing to them the hidden things in which all Israel had gone astray. He unfolded before them his holy Sabbaths and his glorious feasts, the testi-

monies of his righteousness and the ways of his truth, and the desires of his will which a man must do in order to live. (Damascus Document 3:12–16)

What sets the Qumran community apart from the rest of Israel according to this passage is the correct interpretation of the Torah. In typical sectarian fashion, the author claims that the community had access to knowledge and insights that were unique to this group. The origin of this knowledge, according to our text, is not clever biblical interpretation but divine revelation. God chose to reveal these insights exclusively to the community. The subject of these revelations is "the hidden things," a phrase taken from Deuteronomy 29:29. The biblical expression becomes code language at Qumran for the sectarian interpretations of the Torah that became the legal foundation for the group's identity. The passage then goes on to list a few legal issues that were of particular importance, such as the proper observance of the Sabbaths and the holidays. The latter is an allusion to the disputes over the calendar, one of the reasons why the community went into self-imposed exile in the first place. The Damascus Document claims, then, that the Qumran community was founded when God chose these specific individuals and singled them out, entered into a covenantal relationship with them, and revealed to them the *correct* interpretation of the Torah, which in turn sets them apart from the rest of Israel, and which alone leads to life.

The same sentiment is expressed in another text from Qumran, a text variously known as the Halakhic Letter, or 4QMMT. This heavily fragmented text takes the form of a letter, supposedly written by the head of the Qumran community, that was sent to a religious authority, presumably the high priest in Jerusalem, in which the sender explains in some detail the reasons for the community's split from Jerusalem. At the core of the letter is a list of some seventeen legal disputes. For each of them, the author explains how their viewpoint differs from that of the addressee's. The letter ends with an appeal for the recipient to reexamine and properly study the Torah, the Prophets, and David (that is, the Psalms) and to come to appreciate that the sectarian interpretation of the Bible alone is, in fact, accurate. Legal disputes over the correct interpretation of the Torah were the principal reason why the Qumran community went into their self-imposed exile. Some scholars have proposed that 4QMMT strikes a conciliatory tone and that it was written during the early history of the group, when there was still hope that the legal differences could still be reconciled and the community return to Jerusalem, but this is not clear.

Not all of the Dead Sea Scrolls are concerned with legal matters, though. A sizeable number of scrolls belong to the wisdom literature. Some of these wisdom scrolls are copies of texts that had previously been known, while other texts are only known from Qumran. The Torah is not central to these texts. For example, one of the main wisdom texts from Qumran, a composition known as 4QInstruction, never mentions the Torah. But the Torah is mentioned in other wisdom texts. One example is 4QBeatitudes.

> Blessed is the man who attains wisdom, [*gap in the text*] and walks in the Torah of the Most High: establishes his heart in its ways, [*gap in the text*] restrains himself by its corrections, is con[tin]- ually satisfied with its punishments . . . (4Q525 II, 3:3–4; my trans.)

In a long list of blessings, or beatitudes, the author calls on the readers to seek wisdom and to shun folly. Here, Torah is associated with wisdom, much as we saw in the case of Psalms 1 and 119, as well as in Ben Sira 24. Torah is a guide to life; it is not the source of specific legal rulings. Legal concerns are not completely absent from the wisdom texts at Qumran, but they are not central either.

The library from Qumran amply demonstrates the variety of understandings of the Torah toward the end of the Second Temple period. The scrolls show how these different concepts were not mutually exclusive but could coexist side by side.

What Jesus Said about the Torah

The Torah continues to be one of the central topics in the New Testament. We have seen how diverging views about the Torah, its meaning, and its exact interpretation reach back into the Old Testament and proliferated during the Second Temple period. The Dead Sea Scrolls may be the best example of that. Here is a library of texts that reflect a breadth of opinions. Since early Judaism was the home of Jesus and the emerging Jesus movement, it should not surprise to see that the Torah continues to be the subject of debate. This is not a new debate, to be sure, but a direct continuation of the debate we have described above, and it needs to be understood with that history and context in mind. The situation is complicated by the fact that, whereas some of the followers of Jesus were Jewish and came to the faith with their own understanding of the Torah, others were Gentiles who had come to believe in Jesus and who had no preconceived notion of the Torah. This issue is of particular importance for Paul, the apostle to the Gentiles (Galatians 1:16).

I will focus my discussion on Jesus and Paul, who both spoke repeatedly about the Torah, and begin with the first Gospel, the Gospel of Matthew. Matthew wrote for an early group of Jesus followers, of whom a large number were Jewish. Reading through Matthew's story, one gets the strong sense that a concern for contemporary Judaism is always present in his Gospel. It is as if the synagogue were just across the street from Matthew, as it were. More so than Mark and Luke, Matthew feels compelled to address a range of topics that were relevant for Second Temple Jews, among them the obedience to the Torah. One of his central challenges was to convince his fellow Jewish Christians that Jesus was the Messiah of Israel, so that they would not become disillusioned, abandon their newfound faith in Jesus, and cross the street again to return to their previous Jewish lives. In order to do so, Matthew needed to clarify Jesus's position on the Torah.

· The first text I will consider is taken from the Sermon on the

Mount in Matthew 5–7. The sermon, which is the first of five major speeches Jesus gives in this Gospel, is devoted largely to Jesus's understanding of the Torah. The setting on a mountain immediately recalls Moses, the first lawgiver, who went up on Mount Sinai (Exodus 19–24). Matthew describes Jesus as the new Moses: Moses gave Israel the Torah, and now Jesus is about to interpret it.

Jesus's Sermon on the Mount is carefully structured. It is therefore important to understand where in his sermon Jesus explains his views about the Torah. Matthew begins in 5:1–2 by introducing the scene: Jesus ascends the mountain and addresses his disciples. The first part of the sermon, in 5:3–12, consists of nine blessings, or the Beatitudes, as they are commonly called. These are blessings that are intended to console and that promise the faithful a better reality: each blessing begins with a particular aspect of the present reality of Jesus's followers, and the second half makes a promise for their future. The Beatitudes are followed in 5:13–16 by three parables about salt, light, and lamp. In three short sayings, Jesus describes those who seek to live according to the sermon.

At this point, following the eschatological promises in the Beatitudes and the brief characterization of his audience, Jesus steps back and explains his position on the Torah. This is part three of the Sermon on the Mount:

> [17] Do not think that I have come to abolish the law or the prophets; I have come not to abolish but to fulfill. [18] For truly I tell you, until heaven and earth pass away, not one letter, not one stroke of a letter, will pass from the law until all is accomplished. [19] Therefore, whoever breaks one of the least of these commandments, and teaches others to do the same, will be called least in the kingdom of heaven; but whoever does them and teaches them will be called great in the kingdom of heaven. [20] For I tell you, unless your righteousness exceeds that of the scribes and Pharisees, you will never enter the kingdom of heaven. (Matthew 5:17–20)

The passage is looking forward rather than backward. Its main purpose is to introduce the next part of the sermon and to

4) preempt any possible misunderstandings. The fourth part of Jesus's sermon, in 5:21–48, consists of six sayings that are widely known as the antitheses (lit. "oppositions"). They are called antitheses because of their structure: each begins with the words, "You have heard that it was said . . . ," which introduces a quotation from the Torah. To this Jesus adds, "But I say to you. . . ." The so-called antitheses have generated an enormous amount of scholarly discussion about their correct interpretation, not least because their structure appears to suggest that Jesus is here contradicting Moses. That is, the antithetical form of the sayings has been interpreted to mean that Jesus presents a new teaching—a new Torah, so to speak—that contrasts, and some would even go so far as to say flat out contradicts, the Mosaic Torah. This is precisely the kind of interpretation Jesus anticipated in 5:17–20, and which he tried to rule out. What Jesus presents with his so-called antitheses are *not* a set of new legal rulings, and he certainly does not want to minimize, let alone contradict, the Mosaic Torah. Indeed, Jesus articulates *an ideal that does not alter the Torah, but rather radicalizes it.* In his inspirational interpretation of the Torah, Jesus reveals what the Torah is really all about: *the promise of life and the attainment of perfection.* This is why he concludes in 5:48 with this summary: "Be perfect, therefore, as your heavenly Father is perfect."

But we need to return to the passage in 5:17–20. Jesus makes clear right at the beginning that he has no intention of contradicting, let alone of annulling, the Torah. Thus, he begins in verse 17, "Do not think that I have come to abolish the law or the prophets." Here he says plainly that he upholds the Torah and that there is no conflict between him and Moses. He further explains that he has come to "fulfill" the Torah, that is, not simply to obey the commandments to the letter but to perfect the Torah through his life and teachings. In verse 18, Jesus continues in the same vein and places his teaching in an eschatological context by looking to the end of time, when "heaven and earth will pass away." The Torah will last until the new creation. Not even a single letter (the original Greek text reads *iota*, which is the smallest letter in the Greek alphabet), or even the smallest part of a single letter, will lose its significance. Since all of the Torah remains in place, everybody must follow it, and those who don't will be held accountable in the final judgment. There is, in other words, a direct correlation between one's behavior in this world, specifically with regard to one's obedience to the Torah, and one's entry into the world to come. Verse 20, finally, forms the transition to the next section about the antitheses and sums up Jesus's teaching on the Torah in form of a warning: not only are the disciples to obey the Torah of Moses, their righteousness has to exceed that of the Jewish leaders. A tall order.

Righteousness is one of Matthew's favorite terms. By this he means the right conduct in accordance with God's will. The tension in the text arises not from any potential contradiction between Jesus's teaching and the teachings of Moses. Rather, Jesus is asking his disciples to do *more* than obey the Torah, so that their righteousness surpasses that of the scribes and the Pharisees. What exactly does Jesus call for when he requires more than a literal interpretation of the Torah? Later in the Gospel, he addresses the scribes and Pharisees again. Now he is more explicit about what he has in mind.

> Woe to you, scribes and Pharisees, hypocrites! For you tithe mint, dill, and cumin, and have neglected the weightier matters of the law: justice and mercy and faith. It is these you ought to have practiced without neglecting the others. (Matthew 23:23)

Jesus does not rebuke the scribes and Pharisees because they are following the Torah, or because their interpretation of the Torah is wrong. Far from it. Rather, he accuses them of missing the most important part of the Torah, what Jesus calls "the weightier matters of the law." Weightier here means more important, and presumably it also means the more difficult aspects of the Torah. To explain which matters he means, Jesus invokes the prophet Micah: "What does the LORD require of you but to do justice, and to love kindness, and to walk humbly with your God" (Micah 6:8). Jesus does not dismiss or diminish the law in any way, but he does distinguish between more important and less important laws. Following specific laws takes second place behind *intentionality* and *devotion*. Observance alone will not do. The weightier matter is the spirit in which one fulfills the commandments and the recognition that the Torah is about more than individual commandments.

The issue comes up repeatedly in the Gospel of Matthew, most famously when Jesus is asked directly by a Pharisee about the greatest commandment.

> [35] One of [the Pharisees], a lawyer, asked [Jesus] a question to test him. [36] "Teacher, which commandment in the law is the greatest?" [37] He said to him, "'You shall love the LORD your God with all your heart, and with all your soul, and with all your mind.' [38] This is the greatest and first commandment. [39] And a second is like it: 'You shall love your neighbor as yourself.' [40] On these two commandments hang all the law and the prophets." (Matthew 22:34–40)

This brief encounter between the lawyer and Jesus is part of a longer, at times disputatious, exchange between the Pharisees and Jesus, during which they debate a range of religious issues. Matthew's editorial remark right at the beginning of this short scene, that the lawyer was out to "test him," casts a long shadow over the exchange that follows. Did the Pharisee really want to know what Jesus had to say, or did he want to entrap him?

Jesus seems unperturbed. There is nothing polemical about his reply. What is most striking about Jesus's response, apart from its brevity, is how conventional it is. Never questioning the Pharisee's motifs or his proposition that some laws are greater than others, Jesus responds by summarizing two commandments, the commandment to love God and the commandment to love the neighbor. The former is taken from Deuteronomy 6:5, which is part of a traditional prayer in Judaism known as the Shema, a prayer that the faithful recite twice daily to this day. The prayer, which consists of three passages from Scripture (Deuteronomy 6:4–9; 11:13–21; Numbers 15:37–41), is named after its opening line in Deuteronomy 6:5. Jesus is merely reminding the lawyer of what the lawyer knows already. The second commandment, to love one's neighbor, is taken from Leviticus 19:18, "You shall not take vengeance or bear a grudge against any of your people, but you shall love your neighbor as yourself; I am the LORD."

If read out of context, Jesus's response would seem a bit random and his choice of commandment arbitrary. Surely, there are any number of commandments in the Torah he could have quoted. But Jesus's choice may not have been so arbitrary after all. The Babylonian Talmud, a rabbinic work from a much later time, has preserved a short anecdote about Hillel, a famous Jewish leader who lived a generation before Jesus. In this particular episode, Hillel is also put to the test.

> On another occasion it happened that a certain non-Jew came before Shammai and said to him, "I will convert to Judaism, on condition that you teach me the whole Torah while I stand on one foot." Shammai chased him away with the builder's tool that was in his hand. He came before Hillel and said to him, "Convert me." Hillel said to him, "What is hateful to you, do not to your neighbor: that is the whole Torah; the rest is commentary; go and learn it." (Babylonian Talmud, *Shabbat* 31a)

For both Jesus and Hillel, the command in Leviticus 19:18 to love one's neighbor is synonymous with the Golden Rule. And both of these teachers agree that the commandment to love epitomizes the Torah. In Jesus's words, on these commandments "hang all the law and the prophets." Or, in Hillel's words, "that is the whole Torah; the rest is commentary."

Jesus puts the two commandments to love God and to love your neighbor together, since both command to love. They become inseparable, even though Jesus does not explain exactly how the two relate to each other. There is nothing unexpected about Jesus's reply. As Dale Allison, a modern commentator on Matthew, aptly noted, only Christian prejudice will find in Jesus's response a departure from Judaism. Jesus upholds the Torah, and at the same time insists, like Hillel and others before him, that not all laws are equal. The most basic and, at the same time, essential law is the command to love. Jesus's response to the Pharisee, and particularly his reference to "the law and the prophets," reminds us of the Sermon on the Mount with which we began. Already in Matthew 5:17, Jesus declares, "Do not think that I have come to abolish the law or the prophets." Jesus's affirmation in the Sermon on the Mount that he has come to fulfill the law and the twin commandments to love God and neighbor thus belong together. They mark two important moments in the story of the Gospel, and they capture succinctly Jesus's teaching on the enduring significance of the Torah, on the reverence toward God, and on the love for one's neighbor.

What Paul Said about the Torah

The epistle to the Romans is Paul's last letter. It is also the most accomplished exposition of his theology. The apostle picks up and develops further several of the themes and ideas he had previously discussed in his earlier letters. One of the central themes in Romans is Paul's thinking about Israel and the Torah, a topic to which he returns repeatedly over the course of the letter. Why are Israel and the Torah such important topics for Paul?

Paul was born and raised a Jew, who practiced a form of Judaism that he himself associates with the Pharisees. He says as much in his letter to the Philippians (Philippians 3:4-6). He even boasts that he used to be unfailing in following the Torah, "as to righteousness under the law, blameless." Following his famous Damascus experience (Acts 9:1-19), Paul preached that the uncircumcised Gentiles were now incorporated into the people of God. Through Jesus's life, death, and resurrection, the Gentiles are included in God's promises to Israel. The status of the Gentiles is clear: those who have come to see in Jesus the Messiah of Israel now belong to the people of God, but according to Paul they are not expected to become Jews. They are part of the promise, but they are not expected to obey the Torah like the Jews are, circumcise their sons, or follow any dietary restrictions. The main issues that arise from Paul's opening of the promise to the Gentiles concern the current fate of Israel and the significance of the Torah. First, what happens to those Jews who do not share Paul's views about Jesus and who do not confess that Jesus is the Messiah? Does Paul think that they are therefore rejected by God? Second and relatedly, what about the Torah? If the Gentiles become righteous through faith by grace alone, has the Torah, then, become obsolete? What advantage, if any, does Israel have in following the Torah?

Reading through Romans, one can easily get the impression that Paul is here defending himself against his critics and that he is trying to correct their misinterpretation of his position. His opponents could have heard about Paul's teaching or read copies of his earlier letters, such as his letter to the Galatians, of which a significant section is devoted to Israel. According to his detractors, Paul is claiming that God has rejected Israel and that the Torah has lost its theological significance. Paul addresses both of these positions and refutes them one by one—albeit in vain; it appears that Paul lost the argument. Until recently, many of Paul's modern interpreters agreed with his ancient critics. They, too, believed that Paul had effectively converted from Judaism to Christianity, and that as a consequence, Paul had turned against his own people and was now taking Israel to task, disputing the validity of the old covenant, and belittling the Torah. Only in recent decades have scholars taken a new look at Paul and come to realize that Paul rejects neither Israel nor the Torah. A close reading of some passages in the letter to the Romans will demonstrate why this new reading of Paul's letters is correct.

First, what did Paul think of his fellow Jews who did not follow him in proclaiming Jesus to the Gentiles? Did Paul argue that God has rejected them, just as they have rejected Jesus, the Messiah of Israel? Throughout his letter, Paul argues over and over again that the Jews are not excluded from anything but that the *Gentiles have been added* to the people of God. There is only one God, who is, first of all, the God of the Jews, but then also the God of the Gentiles. "Or is God the God of Jews only? Is he not the God of Gentiles also? Yes, of Gentiles also" (Romans 3:29). Abraham is the ancestor not just of the circumcised—that is, of Israel—but also of the uncircumcised, that is, of the Gentiles. The story of Abraham in the book of Genesis gives scriptural legitimacy to Paul's gospel to the Gentiles (Romans 4). And God will save all, not just Israel but also the Gentiles (Romans 11). Paul is consistent in his letter that God has included the Gentiles but has not excluded Israel.

Romans reaches a rhetorical highpoint in chapters 9–11. This is Paul's most detailed reflection on the redemption of the Gentiles and the salvation of Israel anywhere in his letters. For the previous eight chapters, Paul has been working up to this moment, and now he reaches what must be seen as the heart of the matter. Paul opens his treatise on Israel on a deeply personal note.

> [1] I am speaking the truth in Christ—I am not lying; my conscience confirms it by the Holy Spirit— [2] I have great sorrow and unceasing anguish in my heart. [3] For I could wish that I myself were accursed and cut off from Christ for the sake of my own people, my kindred according to the flesh. [4] They are Israelites, and to them belong the adoption, the glory, the covenants, the giving of the law, the worship, and the promises; [5] to them belong the patriarchs, and from them, according to the flesh, comes the Messiah, who is over all, God blessed forever. Amen. (Romans 9:1–5)

Paul addresses the Romans as a Jew. "I myself am an Israelite, a descendent of Abraham, a member of the tribe of Benjamin" (Romans 11:1). We do not know much about the Christian community in Rome, and it is not clear how much Paul himself knew about them. He had never been there before but hoped to visit them soon. Based on his letter, it seems likely that the community consisted of Jews and Gentiles. Two elements in this opening are striking. First, Paul is reaching out to his fellow Jews. The fact that they do not recognize Jesus as the Messiah is painful to him and causes him "great sorrow and unceasing anguish." Instead of turning on them in anger and claiming that they have therefore forfeited their hope for God's salvation, he writes full of longing and compassion. It matters greatly to him that they know that he is writing as a Jew who wishes to convince them and win them over. Paul is not a Gentile who condemns the Jews, he is a Jew who is greatly concerned for his fellow Jews. A little later he writes, "Brothers, my heart's desire and prayer to God for [Israel] is that they may be saved" (Romans 10:1). And second, Paul adds in Romans 9:4–5 a long list Israel's attributes, gifts Israel has received from God that are theirs, among them the giving of the Torah, the promises, and even the messiah. All of these belong to Israel first, and Paul does not claim that God has taken them away. On the contrary, later in his treatise he writes, "I ask, then, has God rejected his people? By no means!" (Romans 11:1). Paul's argument is consistent: God has not taken anything away but upholds Israel's status, and Israel's refusal to believe in Jesus, while the source of Paul's sorrow, does not change any of that.

At the end of his treatise in Romans 9–11, Paul repeats his argument that God's many gifts to Israel and Israel's status as God's chosen people are irrevocable. He reiterates what he has said earlier, but now expounds on the significance of Israel's abiding presence for the Gentiles.

> [28] As regards the gospel they are enemies of God for your sake; but as regards election they are beloved, for the sake of their ancestors; [29] for the gifts and the calling of God are irrevocable. [30] Just as you were once disobedient to God but have now received mercy because of their disobedience, [31] so they have now been disobedient in order that, by the mercy shown to you, they too may now receive mercy. (Romans 11:28–31)

Here, Paul tries to make sense of what is causing him so much anguish: Israel's refusal to accept Jesus as the Messiah. Israel's resistance to the gospel makes them "enemies of God," but God's gifts for them, including Israel's election, are nonetheless "irrevocable." How does Paul explain this? His argument runs like this: the disbelief of Israel is not Israel's own doing. But rather, it is God who has made Israel disobedient to the gospel. And God has done so for a reason, in order to bring salvation to the Gentiles. He writes, "But through their stumbling salvation has come to the Gentiles, so as to make Israel jealous" (Romans 11:11). For Paul, Gentiles and Jews were equally disobedient. But just as God answered the disobedience of the Gentiles not with rejection but with mercy, so God will respond to the Jewish disobedience to the Gospel with mercy.

How about the Mosaic Torah? What does Paul say about the role of the Torah? Since Gentiles are not expected to become Jews and follow the commandments, does this mean the end of the Torah? Here, too, Paul is unambiguous. He addresses the issue in Romans 3, where he asks the question with which we began our chapter: has the Torah been abolished?

> Do we then overthrow the law by this faith? By no means! On the contrary, we uphold the law. (Romans 3:31)

Paul is not interested in rejecting the law. On the contrary, he wants to uphold it. This, then, raises the crucial question: how about the faith of the Gentiles? Does it not render the law obsolete? Paul has already answered this question a few verses earlier.

> [21] But now, apart from the law, the righteousness of God has been disclosed, and is attested by the law and the prophets, [22] the righteousness of God through faith in Jesus Christ for all who believe. (Romans 3:21–22)

For the interpreters of Paul who have claimed that Paul dismisses the law, law and faith are mutually exclusive. For Paul, they argue, the righteousness of God comes either through the law or through faith, but it cannot come through both. Since the law of Moses came first and faith through Christ second, the latter has effectively canceled out the former. In Paul's own words, faith has overthrown the law.

The problem with this reading is that Paul himself makes clear that law and faith are, in fact, *not* contradictory terms.

In the passage just quoted, Paul explains that the law and the prophets already bore witness to the righteousness of God "apart from the law." The redemption of the Gentiles has already been disclosed in the Hebrew Scriptures. Here, again, we see Paul's repeated emphasis on the *inclusion* of the Gentiles, not the exclusion of Israel. Does faith overthrow the law, as the traditional interpreters of Paul would have it? Paul answers that question in Romans 3:31 with an emphatic no.

We need to consider one last verse that has often been quoted by those who want to argue that according to Paul, God has abolished the Torah for Gentiles and Jews alike. That verse is Romans 10:4.

> For Christ is the end of the law so that there may be righteousness for everyone who believes. (Romans 10:4)

The main problem with the verse is the word "end," or Greek *telos*. What exactly does Paul have in mind when he says that Jesus is the *telos* of the law? *Telos* can have multiple meanings. One of them is indeed "end," in the sense of "cancellation; cessation." This has been the traditional reading of the verse: Christ spells the end of the Torah. This is also how most translations have rendered the verse.

> King James Version: "For Christ is *the end* of the law for righteousness to every one that believeth."

> Revised Standard Version: "For Christ is *the end* of the law, that every one who has faith may be justified."

But this is not the only meaning of *telos*. It can also mean "goal" or "fulfillment." Taken that way, Paul argues that *Jesus reveals the true meaning of the Torah and brings it to its true fulfillment*. Far from rendering the Torah obsolete, Jesus makes manifest the Torah's true goal, or *telos*, which is the righteousness of God for "everyone who believes," that is, for the Gentiles.

Romans 10:4 only makes sense when it is read together with Romans 3:21–22, 31. Paul appeals to his Roman readers to recognize that God's righteousness is, and has always been, available to the Gentiles. This righteousness has been available to them "apart from the law," meaning that they do not have to become Jews. Paul does not dismiss the Jews for their refusal to accept that Jesus is the Messiah of Israel. Even though this is a cause of sorrow for the apostle, that is not the main point. Israel's main failure, according to Paul, is not to be able to see the main goal of the Torah. And so he pleads with them to recognize that the righteousness of God is available to the Gentiles as well, albeit apart from the Torah, and that this righteousness has always been available to them. Christ has revealed the true goal of the Torah.

In the end, Paul's wisdom and the soundness of his argument become evident in the conclusion of his treatise on Israel in Romans 9–11. Having made clear toward the end of chapter 11 that Israel retains its status as God's chosen people and that at the end of time God will redeem Israel *and* Gentiles alike, Paul ends chapter 11 with a doxology, a praise of God's wisdom. His doxology serves as a warning—this time not to the Jews but to the Gentiles. Paul emphasizes that God's ways can never be known to human beings. "O the depth of the riches and wisdom and knowledge of God! How unsearchable are his judgments and how inscrutable his ways" (Romans 11:33). Regretfully, all too often Christians have forgotten these lines and have claimed, erroneously, that God has rejected Israel and abolished the law of Moses. Paul sees it differently. "All Israel will be saved" (Romans 11:26), he writes, and he never mentions any condition that Israel first needs to accept the gospel.

6

The Resurrection of the Dead and Life in the Company of Angels

The Resurrection of the Dead in the Gospels

Rumors are circulating about Jesus as people begin to wonder who he really is. How can he teach with wisdom, and how can he execute these deeds of power? Mark tells the story of Jesus, who has just returned to his home town of Nazareth. Soon after he gets home, Jesus sends out his twelve disciples in groups of two into the surrounding villages and equips them with the authority to proclaim repentance, to exorcize demons, and to heal the sick. The Twelve are now sent to do what Jesus himself had previously done (see Mark 1:14–15). If the disciples in Mark represent the church, which is one way of reading his Gospel, then the point of the story is to create a direct line between Jesus and the mission of the church. Jesus and the church are inextricably linked; Mark's Christology (that is, his teaching about Christ) paves the way for, and leads directly to, his eccle-siology (his teaching about the church).

Soon King Herod hears of the disciples' activities and becomes anxious.

> [12] So [the disciples] went out and proclaimed that all should repent. [13] They cast out many demons, and anointed with oil many who were sick and cured them. [14] King Herod heard of it, for Jesus's name had become known. Some were saying, "John the Baptist has been raised from the dead; and for this reason these powers are at work in him." [15] But others said, "It is Elijah." And others said, "It is a prophet, like one of the prophets of old." [16] But when Herod heard of it, he said, "John, whom I beheaded, has been raised." (Mark 6:12–16; see also 8:27–28)

Even though Jesus is absent from this scene and will remain absent from the story for a short while, the episode is all about him. Rumors about Jesus are coming to Herod's attention. Some say that Jesus is John the Baptist, who has come back from the dead; others say that Jesus is the prophet Elijah; and yet others maintain that Jesus is a prophet, like the prophets in ancient Israel. These speculations about Jesus's identity, even though they all turn out to be false, are not as wild as they may first appear. The first rumor, that Jesus is John whom Herod had executed, is born out of the desire to explain why Jesus can act with such authority, as Mark has already stated twice (in 5:30 and 6:2). Resurrection is here associated with power: the idea that Jesus might be the resurrected John is meant to explain Jesus's extraordinary power. The second rumor, that Jesus is Elijah, is rooted in the Old Testament. The prophet Elijah never died but ascended into heaven on a chariot of fire (2 Kings 2:11), from which he can return at any moment. According to the prophet Malachi, Elijah will come back at the end of time to announce the advent of the messiah (Malachi 4:5–6; Mark 9:9–13). Elijah is the precursor of the messiah, but he himself is not the messiah. The third rumor, that Jesus was a prophet, reflects the view, shared by Matthew and the other evangelists, that Jesus was deeply grounded in the prophetic

148

tradition of ancient Israel. Herod, possibly out of fear and guilt over having beheaded John, goes for the first rumor and chooses to believe that Jesus is *John redivivus*, the Baptizer who has come back to life.

The resurrection of the dead is also the subject of John 11, the masterfully told story about the waking of Lazarus, the brother of Martha and Mary, who died and whom Jesus brings back to life. His story is found only in the Fourth Gospel. Lazarus lived in Bethany, a small town about two miles east of Jerusalem. In the story, Lazarus had fallen gravely ill and soon thereafter died while Jesus was away. By the time Jesus heard of the death of his friend and traveled to Bethany, Lazarus had already been laid to rest for four days, and a smell was coming out of his tomb. When Martha heard that Jesus was on his way, she went out to meet him. The following passage is taken from the very beginning of the conversation between Martha and Jesus upon Jesus's arrival in Bethany.

> [21] Martha said to Jesus, "Lord, if you had been here, my brother would not have died. [22] But even now I know that God will give you whatever you ask of him." [23] Jesus said to her, "Your brother will rise again." [24] Martha said to him, "I know that he will rise again in the resurrection on the last day." [25] Jesus said to her, "I am the resurrection and the life." (John 11:21–25)

When Martha and Jesus meet, Martha is the first to speak. It is difficult not to detect in her words a trace of reproach. "Surely, Jesus, you could have prevented the death of my beloved brother Lazarus, if only you had been here," is what she is essentially saying. "But perhaps, not all hope is lost. You can still do something." Jesus's reply is short and to the point: "Your brother will rise again." Martha is quick to confirm Jesus's statement. "I know that he will rise again in the resurrection on the last day."

This is the moment for Jesus to tell Martha that he himself is the agent of the final resurrection. "I am the resurrection and the life." Throughout the Fourth Gospel, John interprets the significance of Jesus's presence on earth through a string of "I am . . ." sayings. Seven times, John tells a story and then has Jesus interject one of the sayings. The "I am" sayings, a peculiar characteristic of the Gospel of John, are John's way of encapsulating who Jesus is (John 6:35; 8:12; 10:7, 9; 10:14; 11:25; 14:6; 15:1, 5). The reader of these passages is reminded of the call narrative of Moses in the book of Exodus. When Moses asks God what God's name is, God replies, "I am who I am" (Exodus 3:14; see also Isaiah 43:10–11). The "I am" in John alludes to that all important revelatory moment in the history of ancient Israel when God spoke to Moses from the burning bush. These seven sayings are an expression of Jesus's oneness with God the Father, a way for John to say that God is fully present in Jesus.

Neither of these two passages, Mark's brief episode about Herod nor John's story about Lazarus, is about Jesus, and yet they both anticipate what will happen to Jesus at the end of his life. The gruesome death of John the Baptist foreshadows Jesus's own death on the cross, and the reanimation of Lazarus looks to Jesus's resurrection. What matters most to us, however, is that both passages already presume the belief in the resurrection of the dead. According to Mark, whose Gospel is commonly considered the oldest of the four Gospels in the New Testament, Herod agrees with those who believed that John the Baptist had been resurrected, not at the end of time but during their lifetimes. And Martha finds comfort knowing that her brother will rise again "in the resurrection on the last day." The longing for the resurrection of the dead is thus not a Christian innovation. It did not come into the world with Jesus. The people whose rumors about Jesus come to Herod's attention, and Martha, too, already know about the resurrection before they meet Jesus. The belief in the resurrection of the dead is thus another aspect of the Christian faith that the followers of Jesus inherited from the Jews of the Second Temple period.

This chapter falls into three parts. I begin with a look at the motif of the resurrection of the dead in the Old Testament. From there, I move to a small group of extrabiblical Jewish texts that announce and, in some cases, describe the rising of the dead. In the third and final part of the chapter, I will read some early Jewish texts that describe a blessed life in the company of angels, a prominent motif we find in the Dead Sea Scrolls and in the New Testament.

When we follow three basic steps—from the Old Testament via early Judaism to the New Testament—we can begin to reconstruct the origin and early history of the belief in the resurrection of the dead in early Judaism. Resurrection language appears in the sixth century BCE in the writings of the major prophets of ancient Israel. In the prophetic books of Isaiah and Ezekiel, resurrection language is used as a metaphor for the restoration and rebirth of the Israelite community after the disaster of the Babylonian exile. In the language of the prophets, exile is the equivalent of death, and restoration and the return to the land of Israel the equivalent of resurrection. The first biblical text that talks unambiguously about the physical resurrection of a group of specific individuals is the book of Daniel, which dates from the second century BCE. Once we have reached this water-shed moment in the second century BCE and the idea of the bodily resurrection has been introduced, the resurrection of the individual comes to be widely accepted and is expressed in a variety of Jewish texts outside the Old Testament. By the time of Jesus and his followers, the belief in the bodily resurrection of the dead was widespread and commonly accepted. For those who meet Jesus, the expectation of resurrection, which they had inherited from their Second Temple predecessors, is a fixed item in their belief that needs no further explication or affirmation.

Resurrection in the Old Testament

No other book in the Old Testament gives a better description of what it means to be human than the Psalms. Whereas in the Torah and the Prophets, it is God who takes the initiative and speaks to Israel, in the Psalms the believers speak to God. The psalmists reach out to the divine, extend themselves beyond their bodies of clay, and in their prayers reveal much about their own human condition. Some psalmists are jubilant, but most are in dire need of help. They may live during times of war or famine, they may be persecuted, or they may have fallen ill. God has become their last hope, and so they reach out to the divine and utter their cry for help. They plead:

> ⁴ Turn, O LORD, save my life;
>   deliver me for the sake of your steadfast love.
> ⁵ For in death there is no remembrance of you;
>   in Sheol, who can give you praise? (Psalm 6:4–5)

Psalm 6 is a prayer for healing. An unidentified individual turns to God in despair and asks to be healed. This poem takes the form of a supplication (it is still used as a prayer of supplication in the daily Jewish liturgy today): "O LORD, do not rebuke me in your anger, / or discipline me in your wrath. / Be gracious to me, LORD, for I am languishing; / O LORD, heal me, for my bones are shaking with terror" (Psalm 6:1–2). Verses 4 and 5, the passage quoted above, form the central part of the poem. Making his case before God, the psalmist gives two reasons why God should help. First, God should rescue the poet for the sake of God's steadfast love. Noticeably lacking is any statement that the psalmist might be deserving of God's intervention, nor is there a confession of guilt. And second, God should intervene because in death the psalmist will no longer be able to praise God, as there is no memory of God in the netherworld.

The same idea is expressed in Psalm 30.

> ⁸ To you, O LORD, I cried,
>   and to the LORD I made supplication:
> ⁹ "What profit is there in my death,
>   if I go down to the Pit?
> Will the dust praise you?
>   Will it tell of your faithfulness?
> ¹⁰ Hear, O LORD, and be gracious to me!
>   O LORD, be my helper!" (Psalm 30:8–10)

Psalm 30 is a poem of thanksgiving that is recited by an individual after recovery from a severe illness. Verses 8–10 look back to the days of illness when the poet was in dire straits;

it is a self-quotation of the poet's prayer for healing. In death, all humans go down to the pit, where they are effectively cut off from the worshipping community and can no longer praise God. It cannot be in God's interest to see the psalmist die, because then the psalmist can no longer fulfill the main purpose of all human life—to praise God. This characterization of death is typical of the Psalms: the dead descend to the pit, or Sheol, a place of darkness, where they are cut off from the worshipping community. In both psalms, individuals are facing death, and both make their case why God should save them. Their words are sincere. The psalmist of Psalm 6 is not yet out of the woods, whereas the poet of Psalm 30 looks back at the illness, having recovered from it.

The psalms are most striking not for what they say but for what they do *not* say. Even though a number of psalmists are on the verge of death, they never speculate about what will happen to them after they die. Is there a day of judgment? Is there any form of divine vindication? An afterlife? Biblical Israel did not know of the idea of rewards and punishments after death or of an afterlife. At the moment of death, everyone, regardless of social status or merit, descends to the underworld. Psalm 6 mentions Sheol, the netherworld to which *all* living go when they die. It is the place for the deceased, not a dreary place of terror like hell in the later Christian tradition. According to Psalm 6, the netherworld is not a place of punishment. Rather, those who are there can no longer praise God; they are cut off from the living, worshipping community. For the psalmist, death is final. Nowhere in the Psalter does the psalmist mention the resurrection of the dead. Deliverance from the pit is entirely this-worldly.

Resurrection language appears in the Bible in the writings of the prophets during the Babylonian exile as early as the sixth century BCE. In biblical prophecy, resurrection is used as a metaphor for the restoration of Israel as a nation. Isaiah 26 is part of a passage known as the Small Apocalypse of Isaiah. It is a psalm cast in the form of a lament. The poet-prophet recalls that even though Israel was subjected to the rule of the Babylonians when King Nebuchadnezzar invaded the land, took the city of Jerusalem, and exiled its population, the Israelites have always remained faithful to their God.

> ^{13} O LORD our God,
>   other lords besides you have ruled over us,
>   but we acknowledge your name alone.
> ^{14} The dead do not live;
>   shades do not rise—
>   because you have punished and destroyed them,
>   and wiped out all memory of them.
> ^{15} But you have increased the nation, O LORD,
>   you have increased the nation; you are glorified;
>   you have enlarged all the borders of the land. (Isaiah 26:13–15)

The lords with whom the poet begins are the rulers of the oppressors, the Babylonians, whose names the Israelites refuse to utter. In verse 14, Isaiah uses language that is familiar from the psalms. The dead are cut off from the living; they do not rise again. This is the prophet's way of characterizing Israel's enemy, whom God has defeated. The purpose of this poem is to give hope to the Israelites that God will overcome their misery and bring Israel home from exile. Soon the Babylonians will be no more.

A few verses later, the prophet contrasts the fate of the Babylonians with that of Israel. Here the poet is addressing the Israelites directly.

> ^{19} Your dead shall live, their corpses shall rise.
>   O dwellers in the dust, awake and sing for joy!
> For your dew is a radiant dew,
>   and the earth will give birth to those long dead. (Isaiah 26:19)

The contrast between the Babylonians and the Israelites is the contrast between death and life. Whereas Israel's enemies are dead and will not come back to life (Isaiah 26:14), Israel will live again. Verse 19 is a direct response to verse 14. "Your dead shall live, their corpses shall rise" (Isaiah 26:19), the prophet promises. The Israelites will survive the death of exile and will come back to life when they return to their homeland. Isaiah's poem is among the first texts in the Old Testament that uses resurrection language. The context makes clear, however, that Isaiah is not thinking of the fate of the individual believers or the hope for the bodily resurrection of the dead. Rather, the prophet uses the language of "death" and "awakening" as metaphors for the trauma of the Babylonian exile. The glorious promise that Israel's "corpses shall rise," a fitting metaphor for the return from exile to the land of Israel, expresses the promise of return to new life.

Our observation that resurrection in Isaiah is an image for the restoration and rebirth of the Israelite community after the Babylonian exile finds further support from a roughly contemporary text, Ezekiel's famous vision of the valley of dry bones in Ezekiel 37. The prophet Ezekiel was taken into the Babylonian exile with the first wave of exiles early in the sixth century BCE, where he remained well-informed about the events in Judah. His visions concern both the expatriates who are with him in exile and those who were left behind in the land of Israel. The vision of the valley of dry bones in chapter 37 was written roughly at the same time Isaiah wrote his poem, perhaps slightly earlier. In his vision, Ezekiel is brought "by the Spirit of the LORD" to a valley filled with bones. There God commands Ezekiel to prophesy to the bones that they shall live again, as God will put new breath in them. When the prophet begins to prophesy, he sees how the bones are coming together and sinews are put on them. The vision itself is then followed by an interpretation.

[11] Then [God] said to me, "Mortal, these bones are the whole house of Israel. They say, 'Our bones are dried up, and our hope is lost; we are cut off completely.' [12] Therefore prophesy, and say to them, Thus says the LORD God: I am going to open your graves, and bring you up from your graves, O my people; and I will bring you back to the land of Israel. [13] And you shall know that I am the LORD, when I open your graves, and bring you up from your graves, O my people. [14] I will put my spirit within you, and you shall live, and I will place you on your own soil; then you shall

know that I, the LORD, have spoken and will act," says the LORD. (Ezekiel 37:11–14)

The passage resembles the poem in Isaiah in that it, too, intends to give hope to the Israelites who are in exile. According to verse 11, the rather striking image of the dry bones that are about to be brought back to life is itself taken from a complaint by the exiles, who had previously mourned, "Our bones are dried up, and our hope is lost." While in exile, the people of Israel had lost all hope, and their exile had become their grave. The divine prophecy to bring Israel "up from your graves" is the equivalent to the promise that God will "place you on your own soil." Like Isaiah, for Ezekiel resurrection means restoration, the return of the exiles to the land of Israel. The dry bones that shall live again are a metaphor for "the whole house of Israel," as the prophet says plainly (Ezekiel 37:11). Ezekiel is not concerned with the fate of the individual after death. Death and resurrection—even though, strictly speaking, there is no resurrection language in Ezekiel 37—are powerful metaphors for Israel's restoration from the exile. It is also important to notice that these are images in the imagination of the prophets. Nowhere does either Isaiah or Ezekiel claim that the reanimation of the dead is actually going to happen in real historical time. Ezekiel tells us that he was taken to the valley of the dry bones "by the spirit of the LORD." In other words, this is *visionary language* used by the prophet to communicate a religious experience. Isaiah and Ezekiel are not hoping for the raising of the dead but the restoration of the people of Israel to the homeland.

Things are very different with our last text from the Old Testament. The first and only unambiguous expression in the Old Testament of the hope in the physical resurrection of a group of individuals is found in the book of Daniel, in chapter 12. The text was written during the second century BCE, a little less than four hundred years after Isaiah and Ezekiel.

[1] At that time Michael, the great prince, the protector of your people, shall arise. There shall be a time of anguish, such as has

never occurred since nations first came into existence. But at that time your people shall be delivered, everyone who is found written in the book. [2] Many of those who sleep in the dust of the earth shall awake, some to everlasting life, and some to shame and everlasting contempt. [3] Those who are wise shall shine like the brightness of the sky, and those who lead many to righteousness, like the stars forever and ever. (Daniel 12:1–3)

Verse 1 refers to a "time of anguish, such as has never occurred" before. This is an allusion to the persecution of the Jews during the rule of Antiochus IV Epiphanes, a Syrian-Greek ruler, who from 167 to 164 BCE turned his anger against Jerusalem, desecrated the temple, and persecuted the Jews. Antiochus's aggression would ultimately lead to the Maccabean uprising and the establishment of Maccabean rule. We are in the fortunate situation of having two Jewish documents, written at the time of the persecution or shortly thereafter, that inform us of the Jewish responses. One is the book of Daniel and the other are the apocryphal books of 1 and 2 Maccabees. There are some significant differences between their responses. Whereas the book of Daniel advocates for a peaceful form of resistance, the Maccabees chose the armed revolt as their form of opposition, which ultimately led to the recapturing of the temple in the year 164 BCE. Daniel's unarmed opposition relied largely on trusting that those who lost their lives in the opposition to Antiochus would regain it in the resurrection.

Verse 1 mentions the archangel Michael, who is said to arise and fight for the Israelites. The authors of Daniel understood their resistance against Antiochus on a cosmic level, with the angel Michael fighting on their behalf. Verse 2 refers to the resurrection of the dead. Here, as in many other early Jewish texts, resurrection is a reward, God's vindication of the suffering and persecuted. Those who have died during the persecutions will be woken again. Resurrection is tied to God's final judgment. Daniel writes of a double resurrection. Those who have resisted Antiochus will be rewarded with life everlasting, while the sinners will be condemned. Their destinies have already been inscribed in the heavenly book. In verse 3, Daniel singles out a specific group, whom he calls "the wise." These are the teachers and leaders of the group of resisters, who have instructed the faithful to endure and who have "led many to righteousness," as the text puts it. It is very likely, as many scholars have argued, that the authors and final compilers of the book of Daniel considered themselves among these wise instructors. They are promised not only that they will be resurrected. Once woken, they will shine "like the brightness of the sky." In their resurrected status, they will be "like the stars forever and ever."

Unlike Isaiah and Ezekiel, Daniel does not use the language of resurrection metaphorically. The seer is also not concerned with Israel as a whole or with Israel's restoration after a disaster. Daniel singles out a specific group of people, the wise, the leaders of the Jewish resistance to Antiochus, and makes them a promise. He readily acknowledges that some of them will die (and, most likely, have died already by the time this text was written). "Some of the wise shall fall, so that they may be refined, purified, and cleansed" (Daniel 11:35). But their deaths will not be in vain, and they will not be final, either. The wise will rise again. This is the first text in the Bible that promises the physical resurrection of an individual, even though the promise is tied to a particular historical situation, the group that receives the promise is fairly small, and the fate of the rest of Israel is simply not considered. And yet, in this youngest book of the Old Testament, at least one group of Jewish intellectuals found comfort in the belief that the death they were facing at the hand of a brutal tyrant was not final and that they would regain their lives again and shine like the stars forever.

Resurrection in Early Judaism

Daniel's apocalyptic outlook, which culminates in the hope for the resurrection of the wise, is unique within the Old Testament. No other biblical author writes about the bodily resurrection of the dead or makes the promise that the righteous will shine like the stars. But Daniel is hardly unique among early Jewish writings outside the Bible. Compare Daniel's vision with Enoch's encouragement of the righteous and pious. Enoch assures the righteous that even though they experience hardship in their lives and may feel that their postmortem state will be no different than that of the sinners, they will not be forgotten. The passage is taken from the Epistle of Enoch, a text that is roughly contemporary with Daniel 12 or may possibly have been written a few decades earlier, at the beginning of the second century BCE.

> ¹ I swear to you that the angels in heaven make mention of you for good
> before the glory of the Great One,
> and your names are written before the glory of the Great One.
> ² Take courage, then, for formerly you were worn out by evils and tribulations,
> but now you will shine like the luminaries of heaven;
> you will shine and appear, and the portals of heaven will be opened for you.
> . . .
> ⁴ Take courage and do not abandon your hope,
> for you will have great joy like the angels of heaven.
> . . .
> ⁶ Fear not, O righteous, when you see the sinners growing, . . .
> for you will be companions of the host of heaven.
> (1 Enoch 104:1–2, 4, 6; trans. George W. E. Nickelsburg)

The hope that God will raise the dead at the end of history was popular and widespread in early Judaism. A number of authors expressed their hope for the resurrection, though exactly who they thought would be resurrected and how they imagined the resurrection would take place differs from text to text. The texts below showcase some of the various expectations. These texts were written over a period of about three hundred years, from the second century BCE, when the idea of the physical resurrection was first articulated in Jewish texts, to the first century CE, the century that saw the end of the Second Temple period and the origins of the Jesus movement. These are the centuries leading up to and including the lifetime of Jesus. It is important for us to pay attention to the particular historical context in which each text was written, to the extent that this is known to us, and to be mindful that each text expresses a distinct hope for a life after death.

2 Maccabees 7: Resurrection and Martyrdom

The book of 2 Maccabees is part of the so-called Apocrypha, those writings that are found in the Greek translation of the Old Testament, the Septuagint, but not in the Hebrew Bible. 2 Maccabees lays out the events that happened in Jerusalem in the middle of the second century BCE. These were tumultuous times that included Antiochus's attack on the temple and the exploits of Judas Maccabeus. The middle part of the book, chapters 4–10, tells the story of the desecration of the Jerusalem temple. 2 Maccabees 6 and 7 are the earliest martyrdom accounts, or martyrologies, in Jewish literature. Such accounts became popular later on, particularly among early Christians, who wrote numerous martyrdom accounts themselves only a few centuries later. The purpose of the martyrdom account is to encourage the faithful to endure in times of persecution and to set a positive example for others. In this particular case, the graphic account of the brutal murder of the faithful in 2 Maccabees 6 and 7 is undoubtedly intended to validate and legitimize the Maccabean rule.

Second Maccabees 6 is the graphic account of Eleazar, a scribe "advanced in age," who refuses to eat pork (see Leviticus 11:7–8) and whom Antiochus tortures and murders. Second Maccabees 7 is the famous martyrdom account of the seven brothers and their mother. The story is set during the height of Antiochus's persecutions. Like Eleazar before them, the seven brothers refuse to eat pork and are tortured to death, one by one. Their mother dies last of all, having witnessed the deaths of her sons. This is the account of the death of the second brother.

[7] After the first brother had died in this way, they brought forward the second for their sport. They tore off the skin of his head with the hair, and asked him, "Will you eat rather than have your body punished limb by limb?" [8] He replied in the language of his ancestors and said to them, "No." Therefore he in turn underwent tortures as the first brother had done. [9] And when he was at his last breath, he said, "You accursed wretch, you dismiss us from this present life, but the King of the Universe will raise us up to an everlasting renewal of life, because we have died for his laws." (2 Maccabees 7:7–9; New Revised Standard Version)

As the seven brothers are brought before Antiochus, tortured, and killed, the narrator gives each of them an opportunity to give a brief testimony that functions as their oral testament. The second brother begins with a taunt, ridiculing Antiochus for his powerlessness, as his authority is limited to this world only. The divine epithet the brother uses, "King of the Universe," well-known from Jewish prayers, suggests that there is only one true King. The sons accept death willingly, confident that they will be resurrected because of their obedience to the Torah. Antiochus has power over this life only, whereas the God of Israel "will raise us up to an everlasting renewal of life" in the world to come.

In the same spirit, the third son willingly offers his tongue and hands and declares: "I got these from Heaven . . . and from him I hope to get them back again" (2 Maccabees 7:11). Similarly, the fourth son says: "One cannot but choose to die at the hands of mortals and to cherish the hope God gives of being raised again by him. But for you there will be no resurrection to life!" (2 Maccabees 7:14). The mother, finally, encourages her last child with similar words: "Do not fear this butcher, but prove worthy of your brothers. Accept death, so that in God's mercy I may get you back again along with your brothers" (2 Maccabees 7:29).

What gives these Jewish martyrs courage so that they prefer to die rather than to obey Antiochus is their belief in the resurrection. The belief of the seven brothers and their mother is grounded in the confidence that God will not ignore their wrongful deaths but vindicate the righteous and raise them up again at the end of time. God will restore and give back to them what Antiochus has disfigured and taken away. This includes their physical bodies.

The Psalms of Solomon: The Resurrection of the Righteous and the Destruction of the Sinners

The Psalms of Solomon is a collection of eighteen psalms of mixed content that are ascribed to King Solomon, even though there is nothing specifically Solomonic in any of the psalms. The psalms were most likely written in or around Jerusalem in response to a particular historical event, the taking of the Holy City by the Roman commander Pompey in the year 63 BCE. The actual authors of the psalms are unknown, though it is clear from the texts that they were fundamentally opposed to the Romans, who in their view violated the city. The authors also strongly disagreed with the Hasmoneans, who had been in charge of Jerusalem since the Maccabean revolt.

A recurring theme in the Psalms of Solomon is the distinction between the righteous and the sinners. The distinction between the two, which is rooted in the Old Testament, is introduced as early as in the third psalm. In this poem, the psalmist calls on the righteous to remain alert and to remember God at all times. The righteous atone for their sins by fasting and humbling themselves, whereas the sinners stagger through life in blissful ignorance.

> [9] The sinner stumbles and curses his life,
> the day of his birth, and his mother's pains.
> [10] He adds sin upon sin in his life;
> he falls—his fall is serious—and he will not get up.
> [11] The destruction of the sinner is forever,
> and he will not be remembered when [God] looks after
> the righteous.
> [12] This is the share of sinners forever,
> but those who fear the LORD shall rise up to eternal life,
> and their life shall be in the LORD's light,

and it shall never end.
(Psalms of Solomon 3:9–12; trans. R. B. Wright)

The contrasting descriptions of the sinners and the righteous that pervade the Psalms of Solomon serve a didactic function: they are intended to admonish the reader to avoid the path of the sinners and instead to follow the example of the righteous. It seems unlikely that the designations of the sinner and the righteous stand for specific groups in the Jewish community. Rather, these are types that represent different ways of life. One is characterized by carelessness and a lack of respect for God, an attitude that is sure to lead to destruction. The other way of life is thoughtful and recognizes that righteousness can only come from God and lead to life.

The same distinction between sinner and righteous is described in the wisdom books of the Old Testament. The ancient sages already instructed their students to avoid wickedness and to pursue righteousness instead. But there is an important difference between the wisdom texts of ancient Israel and the Psalms of Solomon. Whereas the former are concerned with this life only, the psalms look to the world to come. In the words of the psalmist, the destruction of the sinner is forever, not just a temporary misstep, and God will not grant them life in the hereafter. The reward of the righteous, by contrast, is their resurrection and their place in the world to come. They will "rise up to eternal life" to live in the LORD's light, which shall never end.

The same idea is repeated at the end of Psalms of Solomon 15.

[12] And sinners shall perish forever on the day of the LORD's judgment, when God oversees the earth with his judgment. [13] But those who fear the LORD shall find mercy on that day, and they will live by God's mercy; but sinners shall perish for all time.
(Psalms of Solomon 15:12–13; trans. R. B. Wright)

This passage does not explicitly refer to the resurrection, but the close similarities with Psalms of Solomon 3 leave little doubt that this is what the author has in mind. The focus here is on the divine judgment, that decisive moment when God rewards the righteous and punishes the sinners. Judgment will happen postmortem. The righteous will rise to eternal life, whereas the sinners face their destruction and perish for all time. In both the book of Daniel and 2 Maccabees, resurrection is God's promise for those who have died a violent death, the divine vindication for their wrongful passing. In the Psalms of Solomon, the promise of life after death is a reward for their exemplary conduct and piety, not a reparation for their violent or unjust death. They will live "by God's mercy." For the authors of the Psalms of Solomon, the resurrection of the dead does not appear to be the answer to a particular violent threat. Instead, it is a reward for all who follow the example of the righteous and pursue righteousness in their lives.

1 Enoch 51: Resurrection and the Advent of the Messiah

The resurrection motif appears again in the Enochic Book of Parables, a Jewish apocalypse attributed to the patriarch Enoch that is now part of 1 Enoch (chapters 37–71). The date of the parables has been vigorously debated among scholars, and suggestions range from the turn of the Common Era to the late first century CE. In any case, the parables were most likely written about a century after the Psalms of Solomon. Their place of composition is most likely Jerusalem or the surrounding area.

1 Enoch 51 gives a brief account of the resurrection and anticipates the blissful life of the righteous after the day of judgment.

> [1] In those days, the earth will restore what has been entrusted
>   to it,
>   and Sheol will restore what it has received,
>   and destruction will restore what it owes.
> [5a] For in those days, my Chosen One will arise,
> [2] and choose the righteous and holy from among them,
>   for the day on which they will be saved has drawn near.

³ And the Chosen One, in those days, will sit upon my throne,
and all the secrets of wisdom will go forth from the counsel of
his mouth,
for the LORD of Spirits has given [them] to him and glorified
him. (1 Enoch 51:1–3; trans. George W. E. Nickelsburg)

This brief passage describes the rising of the dead and the judgment scene that follows. The earth is the repository of the human body. Its task is to keep the body that "has been entrusted to it" intact until the appointed hour. At the moment of resurrection, the earth reproduces the bodies of the deceased. The soil has three designations in this passage: earth, which is the most neutral of the three terms; Sheol, the same word that is used in Psalm 6; and destruction, another word for the netherworld. Immediately following the resurrection, an individual who is called "my [that is, God's] Chosen One" will appear. The Chosen One is one of several terms used in the Parables for the messiah. The messiah is a divine agent of the end time who will appear on earth after the resurrection to sit on the throne of judgment. The messiah has been appointed by the LORD of Spirits, who is God. The description of the judgment scene itself is kept rather short, and only the fate of the righteous is mentioned. The emphasis is on the promise, not on the condemnation. While seated on God's judgment throne, the messiah will also dispense "the secrets of wisdom." We are not further told what these secrets are, though it seems likely that they are related to the act of judging.

Chosenness is a central theme in the Enochic Book of Parables. The messiah himself is called the Chosen One, and he will sit on the throne to "choose the righteous." The resurrection is no longer an isolated event. It happens just before the advent of the messiah, and like in Daniel 12 and the Psalms of Solomon, it is tied to the great judgment. In Daniel 12, some are raised to everlasting life and others to everlasting contempt, but there is no specific judgment scene. In the Psalms of Solomon, God is the supreme Judge who "oversees the earth with his judgment." In the Enochic Book of Parables, it is the

165

messiah judge who sits on God's throne, having been glorified by God.

4 Ezra 7: Resurrection and the Apocalyptic Drama of the End Time

The apocalypse known as 4 Ezra was written in the late first century CE, a generation or two after the destruction of the Jerusalem temple. It was the loss of the temple that caused the author to write this text in the first place. The author struggled to make sense of the Roman aggression and worked hard to reconcile the recent historical events with God's promises for Israel. Since 4 Ezra was written in the late first century CE, it is, strictly speaking, not part of Second Temple literature (since the temple was destroyed in the year 70 CE, and 4 Ezra was written after the destruction). And yet, much of the material we find in 4 Ezra is considerably older than the compositional date of the book itself. Also, the worldview of 4 Ezra, its language, and many of the questions it raises are very similar to what we find in the Jewish writings from prior to the year 70 CE. Finally, what makes 4 Ezra so fascinating from a Christian point of view is precisely its proximity to the writings of the New Testament, particularly to the Gospels, both in terms of its date of composition and its content.

The passage below is taken from chapter 7. Ezra, the protagonist of the book, is in dialogue with an angel, who speaks on behalf of God and announces to Ezra what will happen at the end of the age. In this passage, the resurrection is one in a sequence of events that have been preordained by God.

> [26] For behold, the time will come, when the signs which I have foretold to you will come. . . . [28] For my Messiah shall be revealed with those who are with him, and he shall make rejoice those who remain for four hundred years. [29] And after these years my son the Messiah shall die, and all who draw human breath. [30] And the world shall be turned back to primeval silence for seven days, as it was at the beginnings; so that no one shall be left.

^{31} And after seven days the world, which is not yet awake, shall be roused, and that which is corruptible shall perish. ^{32} And the earth shall give back those who are asleep in it, and the dust those who rest in it; and the treasuries shall give up the souls which have been committed to them. ^{33} And the Most High shall be revealed upon the seat of judgment, and compassion shall pass away, mercy shall be made distant, and patience shall be withdrawn; ^{34} but only judgment shall remain, truth shall stand, and faithfulness shall grow strong. ^{35} And recompense shall follow, and the reward shall be manifested; righteous deeds shall awake, and unrighteous deeds shall not sleep. ^{36} Then the pit of torment shall appear, and opposite it shall be the place of rest; and the furnace of Gehenna shall be disclosed, and opposite it the paradise of delight. (4 Ezra 7:26, 28–36; trans. Michael E. Stone)

What distinguishes this description of the resurrection from those we have examined so far is that this author has a clear understanding of the eschatological timetable and of the exact sequence of events that will unfold at the appointed hour. The eschatological process begins, somewhat abruptly, with the appearance of the messiah. The fact that God calls him "my son" has its origin in the promises made to the Davidic dynasty in the Old Testament (see Psalm 2:7 and 2 Samuel 7:14), as I discussed in chapter 3. It does not need to be understood as a Jewish response to Christian claims that Jesus was the Son of God, as some have argued but can be explained as an allusion to the Old Testament. The presence of the messiah on earth will mark the last installment of history as we know it. The messiah will reign in an interim kingdom that will last four hundred years. Then the messiah and all human beings will die, creation will be undone, and the cosmos will revert to chaos. Here, too, the proximity to early Christian theology is striking. No other early Jewish text outside the New Testament speaks of the death of the messiah. This state of un-creation will last for seven days, an obvious allusion to the first creation account in Genesis 1:1–2:4. Then the current world will be replaced with a new creation. The language suggests that the future age exists already, even if at present it remains hidden.

The first event in the future age is the resurrection of the dead. The underlying idea is this: at the moment of death, the body and soul of the deceased are separated, the body is laid to rest in the ground, and the soul is kept in specially designed heavenly treasuries. In 4 Ezra, resurrection means the reunification of body and soul: the earth shall yield what it was entrusted to keep intact, much as we have seen in the Enochic Book of Parables. At the same time, the treasuries that are in heaven will be opened, and the person will be restored. Finally, God the Most High will sit on the judgment throne. Pit and furnace await the wicked, and the paradise of delight the fortunate.

The few texts we have surveyed only represent a sample of the early Jewish writings that mention the resurrection. And yet, they show how prominent the hope for the resurrection was in the Jewish imagination. Read together, these passages allow us to draw some very tentative conclusions about the origin and early history of the belief in the resurrection. In the book of Daniel and 2 Maccabees, resurrection is a promise that is made to a specific group and in response to a concrete historical crisis: Antiochus's persecution of the Jews. Their authors made no claim about the fate of all of Israel, let alone about humanity in general. The modern reader is well advised to respect their silence, especially the reader who might wonder what the Old Testament has to say about the physical resurrection of the dead. The fate of all of humanity was simply not a concern for these authors. As time went on, the promise became less restricted, and resurrection was increasingly seen as part of the final drama, one of the events that will unfold at the end of time as God has preordained them. Other events came to be associated with the resurrection, such as the Advent of the messiah. The final judgment came to be described in greater detail. By the first century CE, the time of Jesus and the early formation of rabbinic Judaism, hope for the rising of the dead had become a fixed part of Jewish end time expectations and found a variety of expressions. Given these general developments, it does not surprise to find that some early Jewish authors went even further in their specula-

tion about the future age and started to write about the blissful
life in the company of angels.

Resurrection and the Life in the Company of Angels

The book of 2 Baruch is a Jewish apocalypse from the late
first century of the common era. Like 4 Ezra, to which it is
closely related, it was written after the Roman destruction of
the Jerusalem temple in the year 70 CE. The book takes the
form of an extended dialogue between Baruch, who in the
Hebrew Bible is Jeremiah's scribe and confidant but who in our
text has become a prophet in his own right, and God. Trauma-
tized by the recent destruction of the temple, Baruch inquires
about the meaning of the aggression and the future of Israel.
Now the dialogue turns to the question of the resurrection.
Baruch wants to know in what body the dead will be resurrected.

> [2] Indeed, in what shape will those live who live in your day? Or
> how will the splendor of those persist who [will be] after then? [3]
> Will they indeed then take this form of the present, and will they
> put on these members of chains, those that are now [steeped]
> in evils and through which evils are wrought? Or will you per-
> haps change these, those that are in the world, as also the world
> [itself]? (2 Baruch 49:2-3; trans. Matthias Henze)

Baruch finds it difficult to believe that, since the human body is
"[steeped] in evil" and a constant source of sin, God would resurrect the dead in the same body. Since the world will be transformed, and what is perishable now will be imperishable then,
will not the same be true of the human body? At this point, God
gives a detailed answer.

> [2] For surely the earth will then return the dead, which it now
> receives to preserve them, while not changing anything in their
> form. But as it has received them, so it returns them, and as I
> have handed them over to it, so too it will restore them. [3] For
> then it will be necessary to show to the living that the dead are

living again and that those have come [back] who had been gone. (2 Baruch 50:2-3; trans. Matthias Henze)

God explains that the earth will safeguard the bodies with which it has been entrusted. The resurrected body will be identical to the body at the moment of death, so that those who happen to be alive on the day of the resurrection will recognize the resurrected. Initially, the resurrected will assume the same body they had during their earthly lives. But this is not all.

> ⁷ But to those who have been saved by their works,
> and to those for whom the Torah now is hope,
> and understanding is an expectation,
> and wisdom is faith,
> to them marvelous things will appear in their time.
> ⁸ For they will see that world which is now invisible to them,
> and they will see a time which is now hidden from them.
> ⁹ And time will no longer make them older.
> ¹⁰ For on the summits of that world they will live,
> and they will be like the angels,
> and they will be deemed equal to the stars.
> They will change themselves into any shape they wish,
> from comeliness into beauty
> and from light into glorious splendor.

> ¹¹ There the expanses of Paradise will be spread out before them. And they will be shown the comeliness of the majesty of the living creatures that are beneath the throne, as well as all the armies of the angels who are now held by my word, lest they reveal themselves, and who are held by the command, that they stand in their places until their advent will come. ¹² And then the righteous will be more excellent than the angels." (2 Baruch 51:7-12; trans. Matthias Henze)

Resurrection is here tied to judgment. The fortunate will live "on the summits" of the new world, and they will "be like the angels . . . equal to the stars," a clear reference to Daniel 12. Verse 7 lists the preconditions one needs to meet in order to be counted among the fortunate: good works, Torah obedience, having understanding and wisdom. The righteous who possess all of these will gain entry into the next world. The world to come, together with all its heavenly beings, exists already, our text makes clear, even though it is now "invisible," or "hidden" from sight and will only be revealed at the end of time, when God releases the "armies of the angels." Notice in verse 8 the parallelism between the "world which is now invisible" and the "time which is now hidden." The world to come is thought of in both spatial and temporal terms, and the two become synonymous. Then, when those who are now held back by God's command are released, the rewards will be plenty: originally resurrected in their earthly bodies, the righteous will be like the angels and "deemed equal to the stars" (v. 10); then they will be able to change themselves into any shape or form they want (v. 10) and live in the "expanses of Paradise" (v. 11), together with all heavenly creatures, beneath the throne of God (v. 11), until, in the end, they will be even "more excellent than the angels" (v. 12).

Before we move on to the texts from Qumran, we need to take a quick look at the New Testament and read a few lines from Paul's first letter to the Corinthians. There in chapter 15, Paul writes a marvelous tractate on the resurrection of the dead, the longest and most extensive exposition on the subject in the New Testament. Paul tells his readers right at the beginning that he feels compelled to respond directly to those in Corinth who either do not believe in the resurrection at all, or who, as Paul would have it, are misguided in their thinking about how exactly the resurrection will unfold. It turns out that the author of 2 Baruch was not the only one who was concerned about the corporeal continuity between this world and the world to come. Writing his letter in the 50s, about half a century before the author of Second Baruch, Paul had already responded to the exact same concern. Instead of asking the question himself, though, Paul quotes an anonymous voice, only to go on and dismiss the questioner.

35 But someone will ask, "How are the dead raised? With what kind of body do they come?" 36 Fool! What you sow does not come to life unless it dies. (1 Corinthians 15:35–36)

The author of 2 Baruch is rather gracious in his response and has God give a detailed response to Baruch's inquiry. God walks Baruch through the consecutive stages of the bodily transformation of the resurrected, beginning with the earthly body and the recognition motif, and ending with the state of the resurrected that is "more excellent than the stars." Paul, on the other hand, is somewhat dismissive, at least initially. Then goes on to answer the question with the help of an analogy between the resurrection and sowing.

> [42] So it is with the resurrection of the dead. What is sown is perishable, what is raised is imperishable. [43] It is sown in dishonor, it is raised in glory. It is sown in weakness, it is raised in power. [44] It is sown a physical body, it is raised a spiritual body. If there is a physical body, there is also a spiritual body. (1 Corinthians 15:42–44)

Where Baruch sees continuity from this world to the next, Paul sees discontinuity. Both would agree that the principal difference between this world and the next is that this world is plagued by weakness, decay, and death, whereas illness and death will no longer exist in the world to come. In the words of Baruch, "time will no longer make [the righteous] older" (2 Baruch 51:9). Death will be no more, and the present physical body will be replaced by a spiritual body. Beyond that, Paul remains a bit terse. At the time of the resurrection, Paul writes, *all* will be changed—the resurrected as well as those who happen to be alive at the time. A few verses later he adds, "For the trumpet will sound, and the dead will be raised imperishable, and we will be changed. For this perishable body must put on imperishability, and this mortal body must put on immortality" (1 Corinthians 15:52–53). There are many more significant similarities between Paul and 2 Baruch worth exploring that demonstrate that early Jewish and Christian thinking about the resurrection, as well as about a host of other issues, are not as far apart from each other as is sometimes claimed.

The community that wrote the Dead Sea Scrolls was an apocalyptic group that believed that they lived at the end of time.

They spent much energy on getting ready for that appointed hour when God will intervene and bring history to an end. In fact, they were such end-time enthusiasts that they did whatever they could to pull the world to come a little closer to themselves. It would seem, then, that the resurrection of the dead would be a much-discussed topic at Qumran. And yet, that is not what we find. Several manuscripts of the books of Daniel and 1 Enoch were found at Qumran, which means that the community knew of the resurrection. Beyond that, two other, non-scriptural texts express a belief in the resurrection. One is a short text known as the Messianic Apocalypse (4Q521) that I discussed in chapter 3. It lists a number of events that will happen at the Advent of the messiah, among them the raising of the dead. The other text, known today as Pseudo-Ezekiel because it is closely modelled after the biblical book of the prophet Ezekiel, offers an interpretation of chapter 37 in Ezekiel that I discussed above. However, neither of these two texts is certain to have been written by the Dead Sea community. Indeed, it seems much more likely that they were originally composed somewhere else and then brought to Qumran, which would imply that they do not express the beliefs of the community.

Things are different with the next text, which was certainly composed at Qumran. This is a text from Cave 1 that contains a number of Hymns of Thanksgiving, or in Hebrew, Hodayot. In two of these hymns, the poet praises God for having raised him out of the dust to heaven and for having granted him a place in the company of angels. The text below is the second, slightly longer passage.

> [6] I thank you, O my God, that you have acted wonderfully with dust, and with a creature of clay you have worked so very powerfully. What am I that [7] you have [inst]ructed me in the secret counsel of your truth, and that you have given me insight into your wondrous deeds, that you have put thanksgiving into my mouth, pr[ai]se upon my tongue, [8] and (made) the utterance of my lips as the foundation of jubilation, so that I might sing of your kindness and reflect on your strength all [9] the day. Contin-

ually I bless your name, and I will recount your glory in the midst of humankind. In your great goodness [10] my soul delights. I know that your command is truth, that in your hand is righteousness, in your thoughts [11] all knowledge, in your strength all power, and that all glory is with you. In your anger are all punishing judgments, [12] but in your goodness is abundant forgiveness, and your compassion is for all the children of your good favor. For you have made known to them the secret counsel of your truth, [13] and given them insight into your wonderful mysteries. For the sake of your glory you have purified a mortal from sin so that he may sanctify himself [14] for you from all impure abominations and from faithless guilt, so that he might be united with the children of your truth and in the lot with [15] your holy ones, so that a corpse infesting maggot might be raised up from the dust to the council of [your] t[ruth], and from a spirit of perversion to the understanding with comes from you, [16] and so that he may take (his) place before you with the everlasting host and the [eternal] spirit[s], and so that he may be renewed together with all that i[s] [17] and will be and with those who have knowledge in a common rejoicing. (1QHa 19:6–17; trans. Carol Newsom)

The anonymous poet writes his hymn of thanksgiving in the first person. He starts out by giving thanks—"I thank you," in Hebrew *odekha*, hence the name Hodayot—that God has raised him from the dust. As is typical of the Hodayot, the poet uses strong, self-deprecating language to reflect on his experience: he is nothing, a corpse, and a "spirit of perversion," but thanks to God's initiative, and to God's initiative alone, he has been raised, so that he is now fit to praise God. God has also instructed him in "the secret counsel of [God's] truth," a phrase that is repeated in lines 7 and 12. This is code language for the sectarian teachings of the Qumran community, a secret knowledge that alone leads to salvation. The members of the community are "the children of [God's] good favour" (line 12). They are the fortunate ones, because God has singled them out and has revealed to them special knowledge about the divine truth and about God's "wonderful mysteries" (line 13). Of particular interest to us are lines 13–17. The poet uses resurrection language to describe how God has "purified" him and has "united" him with God's "holy ones," a designation for the angels. In the words of the hymnist, he has been raised "from the dust to the council of [God's] truth" that is undoubtedly in heaven.

How are we to interpret this language? According to some scholars, the author of the Hodayot is here describing the moment when he joined the Qumran community. In other words, in the religious experience of our Qumran poet, he has *already* been raised from the dust and joined with the heavenly host at the moment when he became a member of the Qumran community. Having joined the community is equivalent to resurrection. The poet describes his new life in glowing terms: he has been purified by God and hence has become made fit to praise God, he has gained access to God's special "truth" and "wonderful mysteries," all code language for the teachings of our community, and he has been united with the angels. The idea is that the community members lived *as if* the end of time had had already begun during their life time and *as if* they were already living in the company of angels.

Support for this interpretation of the Hodayot comes from another text from the Dead Sea Scrolls: the Rule of the Community, one of the foundational texts from Qumran. There, in column 11, the author describes what sets the members of the Qumran community, who were chosen by God, apart from everybody else.

> [7] To them He has chosen He has given all these – an eternal possession. He has made them heirs in the legacy [8] of the Holy Ones. With the angels He has united their assembly, a community. They are an assembly built up for holiness, an eternal planting for all [9] ages to come. (1QS 11:7–9; my trans.)

The term "a community" here stands for the Qumran community. The context in the Rule of the Community makes clear that the author is not describing something he expects to happen at the end of time. Instead, life among the angels is a present day reality for the Qumran community. I therefore tend to agree with those who have argued that the author of the Hodayot uses resurrection language to reflect on his experience of having joined the community. To him, this was such a transformation, an experience of complete renewal, that the only way to express it accurately was by using resurrection language.

What this interpretation of the Hodayot does not answer, however, is the question of whether this was all there is. Do the Hodayot effectively rule out a more traditional expectation of the resurrection of the dead at the end of time? Was the renewal-of-life experience of those who joined the sect so overwhelming that it basically rendered any concern for life after death obsolete? Surely the members of the community experienced the death of their fellow members (there are large cemeteries at Qumran). It seems that there is a deliberate ambiguity in the scrolls from Qumran. As clear as they are about the unique theological standing of the group in the here and now, the scrolls leave the door wide open for a more traditional understanding of the resurrection at the end of time. Such playful ambiguities are always frustrating for the modern reader who is looking for certainty, but they may be deliberate and reflect a conscious move on the part of the ancient author: the poet from Qumran blurs the line between what has happened already and what is yet to come, and he refuses to think of the religious experience in this world and that of the world to come as complete opposites, as the author of 2 Baruch and Paul did. They wonder about the physical continuity from this world to the next and raise the question of the corporeality of the resurrected. Will the body then be the same as it is now? The poet of the Hodayot tries to blur that distinction and claims instead that he is already living the resurrected life among the angels, while not ruling out the possibility of a final resurrection.

The last text to be considered is found in the Gospel of Mark. In chapter 12 we read of the only encounter between Jesus and the Sadducees in the New Testament, the one Jewish group of the Second Temple era that did not believe in the resurrection of the dead. Josephus writes that the Sadducees "hold that the soul perishes along with the body" (*Ant.* 18.16). In this text, the

Sadducees test Jesus. They tell him a story of a woman who was married to seven different husbands, and then ask him, while mocking the idea of the resurrection, whose husband she will be in the hereafter.

> [24] Jesus said to [the Sadducees], "Is not this the reason you are wrong, that you know neither the scriptures nor the power of God? [25] For when they rise from the dead, they neither marry nor are given in marriage, but are like angels in heaven." (Mark 12:24–25)

When read in the context of Mark's Gospel alone, Jesus's answer makes little sense. Why does he bring up the angels seemingly out of nowhere? Does he wish to imply that procreation will no longer be an issue, just as angels do not procreate? Jesus is here alluding to a much broader, ongoing, early Jewish debate about the life of the resurrected in the company of angels. It is enough for Jesus simply to allude to that debate without going into any details. For us, to gain an accurate understanding of Jesus's reply, it is imperative to be aware of this broader Jewish context.

You Revive the Dead with Great Mercy

"If for this life only we have hoped in Christ, we are of all people most to be pitied" (1 Corinthians 15:19). Thus writes the apostle Paul to the Corinthians. Paul addresses those in Corinth who, like many progressive Christians today, doubt that there is a resurrection. The Christian faith is not just about this world, Paul retorts adamantly. If it were, then Christians should be pitied most of all people. Without the resurrection, Jesus would not have been raised. And "if Christ has not been raised, your faith is futile" (1 Corinthians 15:17). Paul is uncompromising. The resurrection is essential. The Christian faith is not just about this life.

It was Paul's understanding that he lived at the end of the age in that short time window in between the resurrection of Jesus and the general resurrection, which he thought was imminent. For him, "the ends of the ages have come" (1 Corinthians 10:11) with the death and resurrection of Jesus. Paul calls Jesus's resurrection "the first fruits of those who have died" (1 Corinthians 15:20). He means by this that the end time has already arrived, and the world to come began when Jesus rose from the dead. The resurrection of all believers was just around the corner. It was Paul's expectation that he would live to see the return of Jesus and experience firsthand the resurrection of the dead. And so he explains in his first letter to the Thessalonians what will happen at Jesus's return. "Then we who are alive, who are left, will be caught up in the clouds together with [the resurrected] to meet the Lord in the air; and so we will be with the Lord forever" (1 Thessalonians 4:17). For Paul, the future age was close. It had already been inaugurated with the death and resurrection of Jesus, and it would break in at any moment.

The expectation that God will raise the faithful at the end of time developed during the Second Temple era. It continues to be a part of Judaism and Christianity today and has a fixed part in their respective liturgies. The Amidah, also known as the *Shemoneh Esrei*, is one of the central prayers in Judaism, whose origins may reach back all the way to the Second Temple period. It consists of nineteen blessings. The second of the nineteen blessings is called *gevurah* (might). It describes the powers that are only God's. Chief among the divine attributes is God's power over life and death.

> You, O LORD, are mighty forever, you revive the dead, you have the power to save. You sustain the living with loving kindness, you revive the dead with great mercy, you support the falling, heal the sick, set free the bound and keep faith with those who sleep in the dust. Who is like you, O doer of mighty acts? Who resembles you, a king who puts to death and restores to life, and causes salvation to flourish? And you are certain to revive the dead. Blessed are you, O LORD, who revives the dead.

This petition, known in Hebrew as the *tehiyyat ha-metim* (the resurrection of the dead), is dense with language extolling God the sustainer of life. God supports the falling, heals the sick, and sets the bound free. No other attribute is more emphasized than that of God the reviver of the dead. Five times does this short passage affirm the belief in the resurrection of the dead. Jews and Christians today are united in their prayer, "Blessed are you, O LORD, who revives the dead."

7

Epilogue

What Difference Does It Make That Jesus Was a Jew?

A little over a year ago, as I began to write first drafts for this book, Sharon, one of my undergraduate students, came to see me during office hours. As she sat down and pulled out her paper we were about to discuss, she asked me what I was working on. I told her that I was writing a book on the Jewish world of the New Testament. The main argument of the book, I explained to her, was this: since Jesus and his followers were deeply rooted in the Judaism of their time, modern readers of the New Testament need to have at least a rudimentary knowledge of that Judaism in order to be able to make sense of Jesus's life and teachings. This knowledge won't come from studying the Old Testament. The books of the Old Testament were written hundreds of years earlier, and their religion is therefore not the Judaism of Jesus. Sharon looked at me with amazement. "You don't need a book to know *that*," she replied, somewhat incredulously. "Is there anything so controversial about that that such a book is needed?" What her facial expression communicated to me was something like this: your colleagues don't write books about the earth being round rather than flat, so why are you writing a book about the fact that Jesus was a Jew?

While working on this book over the last year, my thoughts have often wandered back to that moment in my office and the skeptical look on Sharon's face. Why make the case for something that seems self-evident, even banal? Why write a book about Jesus the Jew, when, as Sharon put it, there really is nothing controversial about this? Frankly, why argue about something that is not in question?

But what is self-evident to Sharon is not self-evident to everyone. Just claiming that Jesus was a Jew is not sufficient. To say that Jesus was a Jew remains just a phrase, unless we understand specifically what Jesus's Judaism is. What matters is that Jesus adhered to and practiced a specific form of Judaism, not simply that he was a Jew. Not many readers of the New Testament today know where to turn and what to read to educate themselves about the Judaism of Jesus. They may have heard of the Dead Sea Scrolls and perhaps even of some of the other ancient Jewish writings, but not many will have actually read any of these texts, let alone be able to articulate what these texts can (and cannot) tell us about the early Jesus movement. As I explained to Sharon that day, less than a century ago, New Testament scholars in Germany were hard at work trying to demonstrate that Jesus was not really Jewish, because he was from Galilee; or that he was Jewish in the beginning, but then somehow overcame his Jewishness; or that he sought to reform a corrupt and degenerate form of Judaism, purging it of its excessive legalism and reliance on works. Clearly those scholars had a particular agenda: to deny outright that Jesus was Jewish, or at least to drive a wedge between Jesus and his Judaism. It is not all that long ago that these scholars were active. Some of them were among the top of their field, and their scholarship is still being used today.

As happens often during my office hours, the conversation with Sharon turned out to be more eye-opening for me than it was for her. I am always amazed how my conversations with my students bring as much clarity to me as they bring to them. In talking to Sharon and seeing the doubtful expression on her face, I realized that I had yet to tackle the most fundamental question of my project: so what? It is one thing to go through the rich ancient library of Jewish texts and demonstrate, using specific passages from these books and putting them side by side with the equivalent passages in the New Testament, how the Jewish world of Jesus comes to life through this juxtaposition. But it is quite a different matter to explain what exactly is at stake in this comparison. Does it really make a difference to acknowledge that Jesus was a practicing Jew? And if it does, how so? How does our reading of the New Testament change when we take the Jewish world of Jesus seriously? What are the consequences when we acknowledge that our reading of the New Testament is incomplete at best, and misleading at worst, unless we read it with an understanding of the specific historical and religious context in which it was written, the Judaism of the Second Temple period?

Too Much Judaism? Three Objections

Since I started working on this book, I have given numerous talks on different aspects of Jesus's Judaism to a variety of church groups from different denominations. The great majority of my audiences were intrigued and eager to discover the Jewish world of the New Testament. Their curiosity about this intriguing, yet largely unknown world is often mixed with a sense of relief to find that the differences between Jews and Christians are not as stark as they are often made out to be. But there were also those in the audience who were uncomfortable and felt that there was "too much Judaism" in my presentations. These skeptics have helped me better understand the resistance to the kind of approach to the New Testament I am proposing. They have also brought into focus for me what is at stake in this new awareness of Israel's abiding presence in the New Testament. Our discussions often circled back to one of the following three questions.

1. "How can you say that Jesus was not Christian? He is the source of Christianity. That's absurd!" This is not really a question but rather a reproach, and I have heard it often. It can be difficult for Christians to accept that Jesus was not a Christian like them but, unlike them, was Jewish and deeply absorbed in a set of beliefs and practices that are unfamiliar to contemporary Christians. Christianity as we know it today did not exist at the time of the New Testament. There were those who had come to believe that Jesus was the Messiah of Israel, but Christianity as a religion distinct from Judaism only emerged centuries later.

When I point out in my presentations that Jesus was a Jew, not a Christian, some people invariably feel that I am here to take "their" Jesus away from them. I was invited to speak at their church to make the unfamiliar familiar. My task was to explain something in the Bible that they had not known before. But instead I had made the familiar unfamiliar, which is not what they expected or wanted. It is not my intention to take away anything. The point, rather, is to become increasingly aware of the Jewish world of Jesus, a world that is foreign to most Christians today. I want my audience to realize that Jesus was at home in the Judaism of first-century CE Israel and not in the Methodist or Episcopal or Roman Catholic Church of the twenty-first-century United States. Admittedly, being mindful of this historical divide, acknowledging that Jesus was a Jew, and confronting one's own lack of knowledge about Jesus's Judaism is not easy. Still, it is necessary if we want to be true to the witness of the Bible and its historical and religious setting. None of the writers of the New Testament leave any doubt that Jesus was a Jew who lived in first century Israel.

2. "How can you be so sure that the first authors who wrote about Jesus knew these ancient Jewish books that are not part of our Bibles? Hardly anyone knows these texts today, so why should it have been any different in antiquity? Besides, all I see quoted in the New Testament are the books of the Old Testament." There is always an element of surprise when I point out during my presentations that the Old Testament has preserved

only a fraction of the Jewish books that were in circulation at the time of Jesus. Consider the following. Suppose you could travel through time and have a conversation with Jesus. If you asked him, "What did you read last night before you went to sleep?" chances are Jesus would give you the title of a book you have never heard of before.

The library of ancient Israel was much larger than the books that are familiar to us from the Old Testament. I am not suggesting that all of these ancient books were of equal status to all Jewish groups. Some were considered inspired and hence authoritative by some groups, and others were not. But I am suggesting that the Dead Sea Scrolls and other ancient sources make it abundantly clear that Jews at the time of Jesus studied, copied, and transmitted many more books than we have in our Bibles today. What is more, many of the ancient books that never made it into our Bibles are closely related to the New Testament, just as much as, and in some cases even more so than, the books of the Old Testament. They were read and interpreted at the time of Jesus, and they reflect many of the issues and concerns we read about in the New Testament. We are in the fortunate situation that many of these texts have survived and are available to us today. Still, one might wonder how important these texts really were at the time of Jesus. What evidence do we actually have that the authors of the New Testament were familiar with the nonbiblical writings of ancient Judaism? After all, the texts that are quoted in the New Testament come from the Old Testament.

It is true that most of the quotations in the New Testament come from the Old Testament. There are, in fact, only a few cases of direct quotes of, or of unmistakable allusions to, the nonbiblical Jewish writings from antiquity in the New Testament. One example is the letter of Jude with its reference to the myth of the "fallen angels" in Jude 6 and 14–16. My point is not to argue that the authors of the New Testament knew *specific* Jewish books and quoted from them. In other words, I make no claim that the books of the New Testament depend on specific ancient Jewish books and have used them as their sources. That would be a difficult case to make. In other words, I am not try-ing to prove any sort of direct literary dependence. What I have tried to show in this book, rather, is that the world we find in the New Testament is the Jewish world of first-century Israel. That world is not the world of the Old Testament. If we sup-plement our reading of the Bible with some of the extra-bibli-cal texts from Jewish antiquity, we can recover that world and begin to understand it. There is much in the New Testament that would otherwise remain obscure or go unnoticed if not for this comparative reading.

But we can go a step further. Jewish intellectuals who were active during the last centuries before the Common Era intro-duced a wealth of new features, ideas, and literary expressions into Judaism: the institution of the synagogue; the social and religious divisions of Judaism into distinct sects, such as the Pharisees, the Sadducees, and the Essenes; the rabbi as a reli-gious authority; a concern for angels, spirits, and demons; the apocalypse as a distinct literary genre; and an array of theo-logical concepts and concerns, among them the belief in the messiah as a divine agent of the end time, the hope for the res-urrection of the dead, and the angelic afterlife. The list goes on. None of these aspects of Judaism are found in the Old Testa-ment. They took shape during the time of the Second Temple period and became fixed parts of Judaism during the centuries leading up to the time of Jesus. By the time the books of the New Testament were written, these ideas and concepts were taken for granted and no explanation was necessary. The rise of Jesus and his followers would have been unthinkable with-out these remarkable and courageous Jewish thinkers, Jesus's intellectual ancestors, who changed the face of Judaism forever and who inadvertently paved the way for the Jesus movement in the first century CE.

3. "When we read the New Testament side by side with the ancient Jewish literature, are we not calling the singular importance of God's revelation in Jesus Christ into question? Is Christianity no longer unique?" There is a variation of this concern about the uniqueness of the Christian faith that can be

summarized like this: "We all know from the New Testament that Jesus is the Son of God. So what does this have to do with the Jewish books you are talking about, let alone with Jewish books that are not even part of the Bible?"

For many Christians today, the New Testament has no parallel. It simply is *the* Bible. And as the Bible, it stands in a category by itself and cannot be compared with any other writings. Besides, what other writings are there to which one could legitimately and profitably compare it?

The claim that the Bible is a unique document that is without parallel is not new. A little over a century ago, when pioneering European scholars "discovered" the ancient Near East and began to excavate its rich civilizations, entire libraries were unearthed and hitherto unknown documents, written in languages such as Sumerian, Akkadian, Egyptian, Ugaritic, and Hittite, came to light. As scholars began the arduous task of deciphering these languages and reading the newly discovered documents, they soon realized that many of these texts were significantly older than the Old Testament and that the authors of the Bible were familiar with the books and religions of their surrounding cultures. The biblical authors rejected some aspects of the religions that surrounded them and adopted and transformed others. The realization that the Old Testament was not written in a vacuum, but that Israel's ancient library is but a small piece in the much larger mosaic of ancient Near Eastern libraries, transformed biblical scholarship a century ago. All of a sudden, large parts of the Old Testament were no longer unique. The creation accounts in the Bible, for example, were no longer the oldest creation accounts known to exist. The Bible was no longer the only ancient Near Eastern document that tells of a deluge in primordial times or that names the ancient deities Baal and Asherah. And the specific form of the covenant between God and the Israelites was no longer unparalleled, either, but turned out to have been modelled after the ancient Near Eastern treatises that regulated the contractual relations between the emperor of a sovereign state and his vassal kings. Today, reading the texts from Israel's neighboring civilizations is an integral part of modern biblical scholarship, and interpreting the Old Testament within its ancient Near Eastern context has become a standard feature in college textbooks and modern introductions to the Old Testament.

To observe that the Old Testament has a historical and literary context and that it needs to be read with that context in mind does not take away anything of its significance, either as a theological document or as a book that has shaped Western civilization like no other. It merely takes seriously the fact that the books of the Bible were written by people at specific moments in time and in specific historical contexts. In many cases, we are reasonably well-informed about who these people were and about the circumstances in which they wrote.

In considering the New Testament, the subject is different, but the principle is the same. Rather than the ancient Near East, the comparative material comes from contemporary Jewish sources. And rather than the literature and history of ancient Israel, the subject is Jesus and the origins of the Jesus movement. But the idea is similar: the books of the Bible were written in specific contexts, and knowing those contexts is a powerful tool in the toolbox of the modern interpreter. This does not imply that God does not speak through the Bible. But it does mean that even as instruments of God's revelation, the books of the Bible were written by specific authors in specific times, and that it is important, *particularly* for a theological understanding of the biblical books, to be mindful of this context.

Reading the New Testament in this spirit can have the effect of demystifying the sacred text, of turning it into a document that can be subjected to a careful reading like any other ancient text. For some readers this can be eye-opening, even liberating, as it invites them to become inquisitive readers of the biblical text who are encouraged to bring their questions to the text without fear. Yet for others, the same approach can be unsettling, and understandably so. Once we acknowledge that the New Testament has a specific historical and cultural context, much of what we read is no longer unparalleled. Jesus is no longer the only religious authority in ancient Israel who talked about such topics as the law, the Sabbath, and resurrection. Jesus's apocalyptic speeches in the Gospels turn out to be strikingly similar to the early Jewish apocalyptic books that were written a few centuries earlier. And even Jesus's discussions with the Jewish authorities are not unique.

I remember vividly when, as a young student, I first learned about the ancient Jewish culture of religious dispute that was prevalent during Second Temple times. I had always thought that Jesus's heated debates with the Pharisees about various religious matters were unprecedented and without parallel in the ancient world. They certainly were to me! But then I learned that Jewish groups had engaged in the same kind of religious debates for centuries, arguing the same issues without coming to a definitive agreement. I realized that there really is nothing extraordinary about the nature of the disputations between Jesus and the Pharisees in the New Testament. Jesus's interactions with his Jewish interlocutors have to be read in light of this larger and pervasive culture of debate in ancient Judaism, even if that broader context is invisible when all we read are the Gospels. Not knowing the context of the New Testament does not mean that there is no context.

To point out that a text—sacred or profane—was written in a specific historical context does not say anything about the significance or importance of that text, and it certainly does not diminish its value. It merely points out that all texts are written at a particular moment in time and that to understand the text, we need to interpret it first and foremost within that original historical and cultural context in mind. The Bible is no exception.

The most serious objection I have heard along these lines is not the refusal to acknowledge that the early Jesus movement had a specific historical context, however. Few will dispute that. Rather, it is a *theological* objection, and it has deep roots in the Christian history of biblical interpretation. It is the concern for the uniqueness of Jesus and the Christian faith. The pioneering scholars of the nineteenth and early twentieth century who worked on the forgotten books of ancient Judaism, most of them European Protestant theologians, had deeply ambivalent feelings about the ancient books they were collecting and publishing. On the one hand, they saw the benefits of becoming familiar with the long-lost texts. Advocates of a historical approach to the New Testament, these scholars clearly understood that these Jewish texts could shed much light on the nascent Jesus movement. And yet, on the other hand, they also made it very clear that they considered these texts inferior. They kept pointing out that they were not part of our Bibles. The designations they chose to describe them, Apocrypha (meaning "the hidden texts") and Pseudepigrapha (meaning "falsely attributed texts"), are pejorative terms that were picked deliberately to mark these books as somehow less valuable than the biblical books. To these scholars, the point of comparing and contrasting the New Testament with its contemporary Jewish literature was to underscore the superiority of the New Testament.

The comparison between the Jewish writings and the New Testament was not based on a careful reading of the texts or on a critical evaluation of the evidence. Rather, it was based on a theological decision that had already been made: that Jesus was somehow better than his Jewish contemporaries; that nobody else could say or do what Jesus did; that his life and message were unparalleled, regardless of what kind of information the comparative evidence would yield; and that the salvation that is present and available in Jesus is not available, and never will be available, in any form of Judaism. Such a theological stance was necessary, they felt, to preserve the uniqueness of God's revelation in Jesus and to safeguard the superiority of Christianity over Judaism.

In an extreme form, the belief that Jesus was better than the Jews of his time is called supersessionism. Supersessionism, or "replacement theology," is the Christian belief that the church has superseded Israel. God's patience with Israel has run its course. Because "the Jews" have rejected Jesus, God has replaced them with the church, and the church has become the New Israel. Supersessionism often begins with a particular reading of the New Testament that aims to pitch Jesus against his Jewish contemporaries.

Supersessionism, which has been part of Christianity for a very long time, has to be rejected, since it is both misguided and unhelpful. For one, supersessionism has no interest in the living traditions and practices of Judaism in any serious way, nor is it interested in giving the ancient Jewish texts a fair reading. The sole interest of the supersessionists is in asserting Christian supremacy over Judaism. Who is right and who is wrong has already been decided long before any books are opened and any texts are studied. Instead of accepting that Jesus was a Jew, in the supersessionist reading Judaism becomes "the other," that which is outside of, even alien to, Jesus. Judaism has no intrinsic value in and of itself but is relevant only because Jesus has overcome it and has rendered it obsolete.

Supersessionism also imagines a degraded form of Judaism that is depicted in such negative terms that it borders on the absurd. In the supersessionist view, Judaism typically is reduced to a deteriorated form of religion, an unfortunate distortion of what was once the pure religion of the biblical prophets. Its followers are obsessed with fulfilling the letter of the law in the hopes of some divine reward. It goes without saying that this form of legalistic Judaism is a caricature at best that bears no resemblance to anything we know about Judaism of the first century, or of any other century, for that matter. It is equally clear that this way of thinking about Judaism, which is hardly unique to supersessionists, is a source of many forms of modern anti-Judaism. Today, most Christian mainline denominations have renounced supersessionism, though residues of this kind of thinking are still widespread.

Reading the New Testament in the Twenty-First Century: Three Challenges

1) Biblical scholarship experienced some welcome changes in the twentieth century that have begun to alter the ways in which we read the Bible. A number of things have contributed to this positive development, the most important of which, no doubt, was the Holocaust. The murder of six million Jews by the Nazi regime has forced Christians to reconsider whether the grotesque and often stereotypical descriptions of "the Jew" that were not uncommon in pre-Holocaust Christian circles may have contributed to the anti-Jewish sentiments that formed the basis of Nazi racial ideology. As a result of this reexamination, we see a much greater willingness among Christians today to be self-critical and to examine how they talk and write about Jews and Judaism.

2) Another event that changed our reading of the New Testament was the discovery of ancient manuscripts, most significantly of the Dead Sea Scrolls in the 1940s and 1950s. Because of these discoveries, as well as a greater focus on the literature of the Second Temple period, we are much better informed about ancient Judaism, the Judaism from which Jesus and his followers emerged, than we were at the beginning of the twentieth century. The new insights gleaned from ancient texts have helped to correct old stereotypes, and they enable us to gain a more nuanced understanding of the diversity of ancient Jewish groups, and their literatures, beliefs, and practices, before and during the time of Jesus.

3) Third, opportunities for Jews and Christians to meet and interact with one another have increased significantly in recent decades. It has become much more common for Jewish and Christian scholars to collaborate than used to be the case only a generation ago. The faculties of religion, theology, and ancient Near Eastern studies at the major research universities in the United States today include Jews and Christians, who accept Jewish, Christian, and secular students into their PhD programs. Modern methods of interpreting the Bible that are

widely used by scholars and that are accepted by the majority of Jewish, Catholic, and Protestant scholars today level the playing field, so to speak, for a common engagement with the ancient texts. International research projects on the Bible, biblical archaeology, the Dead Sea Scrolls, ancient Judaism, and, more recently, the New Testament typically engage Jewish and Christian scholars who work together. These encounters between Jews and Christians are, of course, not limited to scholars. Non-scholars also benefit from new opportunities for Jews and Christians to meet, through interfaith groups, for example, or in civic engagement projects.

Because of these changes, the twenty-first century opens up new opportunities for Christian readers of the New Testament that were not available to previous generations. This offers new, exciting opportunities to engage the old and familiar texts from fresh perspectives, but it also poses some real challenges. The first challenge for Christian readers of the New Testament today is to become familiar with the rich trove of Jewish texts, some of which I have discussed in this book, that expand our understanding of the Christian Bible. English translations of the Dead Sea Scrolls and of the other ancient Jewish texts are now readily available, and new tools that help the reader make the connection between Jewish texts and their New Testament counterparts are being published apace (I list some of these resources in the back of this book). The challenge is to become an informed reader of the New Testament, to broaden the scope and depth of one's biblical literacy beyond the boundaries of the biblical canon, and to gain familiarity with what may be unfamiliar.

The second challenge for the Christian reader of the New Testament is to stay clear of the traps of supersessionism and of other ideologies that denigrate Judaism—in the classroom, in the liturgy, and in the pulpit. Anti-Judaism has been the cancer of the church for two millennia. Much of Christian anti-Judaism today is rooted in a distorted reading of the New Testament that fails to acknowledge Jesus's Judaism. Here, the challenge for the modern reader is to engage the ancient Jewish as well as the New Testament texts with an open and inquisitive mind and to reject any false, preconceived notions of Christian supremacy.

3)   The third challenge, finally, is to be mindful of the distinction between Jesus and his followers on the one hand and Christianity as an independent religion on the other. It took centuries for Judaism and Christianity to go their own separate ways and to become two essentially distinct religions. Jesus was a Jew, and the early Jesus movement was an inner-Jewish movement. The Parting of the Ways, as the gradual separation process of Judaism and Christianity is often called, happened long after the life of Jesus, as both religions evolved and institutionalized their differences. From what date can we justifiably describe Christianity as a religion distinct from Judaism, with its own fully independent system of religious belief and practices? This is a matter of considerable scholarly debate. Scholars used to point to the late first century CE as the decisive breaking point between Jews and Christians, but most scholars today will claim that the parting of the ways happened much later, perhaps in the second, third, or as late as the fourth century CE. Whatever the case may be, as Judaism and Christianity gradually drifted apart, their differences became more pronounced, and their respective identities more distinct. To some extent, the separation of the two religions was never completed, as Christianity will always be linked to Judaism, for example, through the books of the Old Testament and through some of the most fundamental beliefs examined in this book, such as the belief in the messiah and the resurrection of the dead. After the death of Jesus, those who confessed that Jesus is the Messiah of Israel tried to make sense of his life, death, and resurrection. The belief in the resurrection of Jesus changed the way his followers thought of him. The small movement of Jesus's followers gradually evolved to become Christianity, and Christian aspirations to be "unique" became more pronounced over time. The challenge for the modern reader is not to project these later claims of uniqueness back onto

the life of Jesus, erroneously assuming that the separation of Judaism and Christianity was already complete with Jesus.

Above all, reading the New Testament in the twenty-first century requires humility. Writing only a couple of decades after the life and death of Jesus, the apostle Paul already knew of the tendency of the Gentile followers of Jesus to become arrogant and turn against their fellow Jewish believers. In his letter to the Romans, Paul reflects on the relation between Jews and the Gentiles who had come to believe in Jesus. In chapter 11, Paul uses the allegory of the olive tree to make his case. The Jews are the natural branches of the olive tree and the Gentiles the wild olive shoots from the wild olive tree. God has broken off some of the natural branches to make room for the wild shoots, which God has grafted onto the tree. Now Paul turns to the Gentiles.

> [19] You will say, "Branches were broken off so that I might be grafted in." [20] That is true. They were broken off because of their unbelief, but you stand only through faith. So do not become proud, but stand in awe. [21] For if God did not spare the natural branches, perhaps he will not spare you. (Romans 11:19–21)

The point of the powerful allegory of the olive tree, the apostle makes clear, is to warn the Gentile followers of Jesus not to become boastful and to feel themselves superior to Israel. Since God has grafted them onto the tree, God can also take them out again, just as God has taken out some of the natural branches. Rather than feeling superior to the natural branches, they are to "stand in awe." Christians today would do well to heed the voice of the apostle.

Acknowledgments

No book is written in isolation, and this book is no exception. It is with great pleasure that I express my sincere gratitude to those who have helped me along the way. I would like to thank, first of all, my audiences in the synagogues and churches where I was invited to present portions of this book. I have benefitted immensely from the lively discussions and the feedback I have received. It is with these audiences in mind that I have written this book.

Several colleagues and friends have discussed this book project with me, read parts of the emerging manuscript, and kindly offered their advice. I am especially indebted to Avril Alba, Richard Bautch, M. Eugene Boring, Kelley Coblentz Bautch, Cindy and John Dawson, Robert Erlewine, Jens Herzer, Jon Levenson, Judith Newman, George Nickelsburg, and Melissa Weininger. All mistakes that remain are entirely my own.

I wrote much of this book in the fall and winter of 2016. I would like to thank the Humanities Research Center at Rice University, and its director Farès el-Dahdah and associate director Melissa Bailar, for granting me a Teaching Release Fellowship for the fall semester. In August and September 2016, I was a scholar in residence at the Mandelbaum House, the Jewish residential college on the beautiful campus of the University of Sydney, Australia. While at Mandelbaum, I gave four public talks on what are now chapters 3 through 6 of this book.

I would like to thank the Mandelbaum Trust, and especially Avril Alba, Ian Young, Naomi Winton, Shana Kerlander, and all the Mandelbaum students for their very warm hospitality. I am delighted to be part of the Mandelbaum family.

Neil Elliott of Fortress Press has been an advocate of this project since its inception and has seen it through its various stages to its production. I am very grateful. My wife, Karin Liebster, has listened with great patience to my unformed ideas during many evening walks with Schmitty the dog and has offered her rich insights. It is to her that I dedicate this book with deepest affection. Über allem aber steht, *Deo gratias*.

Further Reading

Following my presentations in different congregations, I have often been asked by members in the audience whether I could recommend some books on ancient Judaism and early Christianity that are written for a general audience. As interest in the Jewish literature of the Second Temple period has grown exponentially in recent decades, a number of excellent books have come out that are tremendously helpful and open up this fairly new field of study to a broader readership. Below are some of these titles, all written by leading Jewish and Christian experts in their respective fields. None requires any previous knowledge or the ability to read ancient languages.

Introductions to the Old Testament

The reader for whom the scholarly reading of the Bible is still unfamiliar territory may want to begin with a modern introduction to the Old Testament. There is no shortage of books from which to choose. I highly recommend James L. Kugel, *How to Read the Bible: A Guide to Scripture, Then and Now* (New York: Free Press, 2008). Kugel, one of the preeminent Jewish biblical scholars today, takes his readers on a fascinating tour through the Old Testament, paying particular attention to the ways in which premodern Jewish and Christian readers interpreted the Bible. Another excellent and equally accessible introduction that is intended primarily as a textbook for college students and seminarians is Michael D. Coogan, *The Old Testament: A Historical and Literary Introduction to the Hebrew Scriptures*, 3rd ed. (New York: Oxford University Press, 2014). I also highly recommend John J. Collins, *A Short Introduction to the Hebrew Bible*, 2nd ed. (Minneapolis: Fortress Press, 2014).

Introductions to Early Judaism

There are several excellent introductions to early Judaism. James C. VanderKam has written a tremendously helpful book on the Second Temple period and its literature, titled *An Introduction to Early Judaism* (Grand Rapids: Eerdmans, 2001). VanderKam first provides a historical overview from the end of the Babylonian exile to the Bar Kokhba revolt, then goes through the ancient Jewish books one by one, and finally writes about the diverse Jewish groups and their beliefs. A classic in the field is Shaye J. D. Cohen's *From the Maccabees to the Mishnah*, 3rd ed. (Louisville: Westminster John Knox, 2014). This is an excellent introduction to early Judaism, written by one of the leading scholars on Jewish antiquity, that focuses on the period from the Maccabean revolt to the rise of rabbinic Judaism. Cohen is particularly insightful in his discussion of the origin and early history of some of the main concepts, ideas, and social institutions in early Judaism. For the reader who is looking for an introduction specifically to the Jewish writings of ancient Judaism, George W. E. Nickelsburg has written the authoritative introduction, *Jewish Literature between the Bible and the Mishnah*, 2nd ed. (Minneapolis: Fortress Press, 2005). As the title suggests, the focus is on the ancient Jewish books themselves, their literary composition, and main subjects.

Special Topics in Early Judaism

There are numerous modern studies that focus on specific aspects of early Judaism on which I have touched only briefly in this book. James VanderKam and Peter Flint have coauthored an excellent introduction to the Dead Sea Scrolls, *The*

Meaning of the Dead Sea Scrolls: Their Significance for Understanding the Bible, Judaism, Jesus, and Christianity (San Francisco: Harper-SanFrancisco, 2004). On the subject of the messiah, Joseph A. Fitzmyer, *The One Who Is to Come* (Grand Rapids: Eerdmans, 2007), provides a thorough but easy-to-follow discussion of the relevant Jewish and Christian texts. Slightly more academic is the book by Adela Yarbro Collins and John J. Collins, *King and Messiah as Son of God: Divine, Human, and Angelic Messianic Figures in Biblical and Related Literature* (Grand Rapids: Eerdmans, 2008). Dale C. Allison's commentary on the Gospel of Matthew, *Matthew: A Shorter Commentary* (London: T&T Clark, 2004), is immensely helpful, for beginner and scholar alike. John G. Gager has written a slender but important book on the "new Paul" that corrects some earlier misreadings of the apostle, *Reinventing Paul* (Oxford: Oxford University Press, 2000). Kevin J. Madigan and Jon D. Levenson, a Christian and a Jewish scholar, have coauthored a beautiful and deeply learned book on the resurrection, *Resurrection: The Power of God for Christians and Jews* (New Haven: Yale University Press, 2009).

Early Judaism and the New Testament

In recent decades, a growing number of scholars have started to read and write about the New Testament from a Jewish perspective. This is a fairly new approach to the familiar texts that has greatly enriched the modern study of the Bible. An exceptionally useful tool in this regard is *The Jewish Annotated New Testament* (Oxford: Oxford University Press, 2011), edited by two leading Jewish scholars, Amy-Jill Levine and Marc Zvi Brettler. Levine and Brettler have assembled a group of Jewish scholars who provide rich annotations on each of the New Testament books. The book concludes with a number of excellent essays on a wide array of topics regarding early Judaism and Christianity. Amy-Jill Levine herself is a veteran in the field of Jewish scholarship on early Christianity. Her book *The Misunderstood Jew: The Church and the Scandal of the Jewish Jesus* (New York: HarperCollins, 2007) is less concerned with Second Temple Judaism and its literatures but focuses on Jesus and modern stereotypes about Judaism. A classic in the field is Geza Vermes's *Jesus the Jew: A Historian's Reading of the Gospels* (London: SCM, 2001). Finally, George W. E. Nickelsburg is a Christian New Testament scholar who has written an important book titled *Ancient Judaism and Christian Origins: Diversity, Continuity, and Transformation* (Minneapolis: Fortress Press, 2003). This is a deep reflection on how the Jewish texts from the Second Temple era can shed light on the New Testament and the birth of Christianity.

Early Jewish Texts in English Translation

Nothing will open up the world of early Judaism like reading the ancient texts firsthand. Three prominent Jewish scholars, Louis H. Feldman, James L. Kugel, and Lawrence H. Schiffman, have recently published a massive, three-volume set of early Jewish texts in English translation, *Outside the Bible: Ancient Jewish Writings Related to Scripture* (Philadelphia: The Jewish Publication Society, 2013). These volumes present annotated excerpts of a variety of ancient Jewish texts, taken from the Bible, the Dead Sea Scrolls, and other important ancient works. Even though the annotations are intended primarily for Jewish readers, the relevance of this important anthology for the New Testament will immediately be evident. George W. E. Nickelsburg and Michael E. Stone have compiled a most useful anthology of ancient Jewish texts in English translations, *Early Judaism: Texts and Documents on Faith and Piety*, rev. ed. (Minneapolis: Fortress Press, 2009). The book includes many short excerpts of the ancient texts, grouped by subject matter.

There are several excellent modern translations of the Dead Sea Scrolls. Geza Vermes, *The Complete Dead Sea Scrolls in English*, rev. ed. (London: Penguin, 2011), is particularly good. My own translations in this volume are based on a more scholarly edition of the scrolls that prints the Hebrew/Aramaic text and the English translation on facing pages: Donald W. Parry and

Emanuel Tov, eds., *The Dead Sea Scrolls Reader*, 2nd ed., revised and expanded (2 vols.; Leiden: Brill, 2014). The translations of 1 Enoch in this book are taken from George W. E. Nickelsburg and James C. VanderKam, *1 Enoch: A New Translation* (Minneapolis: Fortress Press, 2004). The translations 4 Ezra and 2 Baruch are by Michael E. Stone and Matthias Henze, *4 Ezra and 2 Baruch: Translations, Introductions, and Notes* (Minneapolis: Fortress Press, 2013). And the translations of Jubilees and the Psalms of Solomon appeared in a classic, slightly dated but still most useful two-volume collection of Old Testament pseudepigraphic texts, edited by James H. Charlesworth, *The Old Testament Pseudepigrapha* (New York: Doubleday, 1983 and 1985).

Glossary

Note: This glossary explains some of the names and phrases that are commonly used in biblical studies and that I have used in this book as well, but that may not be familiar to the reader.

Alexander the Great (personal name) – This Macedonian-Greek king (reigned 336–323 BCE) conquered the Persian Empire to build an enormous empire of his own, stretching from Macedonia to India. Alexander is important for the study of early Judaism because of Hellenism, the spread of Greek language and associated culture that deeply affected all aspects of Jewish life. See chapter 1.

Antiochus IV Epiphanes (personal name) – A Syrian-Greek ruler whose name means "god manifest" (reigned 175–164 BCE) and who was an aggressive proponent of Hellenism. From 167 to 164 BCE, Antiochus plundered and desecrated the Jerusalem temple and outlawed the religious practices of the Jews. This led to the Maccabean revolt. Daniel 7–12 and 1 and 2 Maccabees were written in responses to Antiochus's aggression. See chapter 1.

apocalypse (noun; adj. **apocalyptic**) – From Greek, *apokalypsis* (uncovering; revelation). A particular literary genre of Jewish and Christian literature in which God discloses some otherwise inaccessible knowledge to a human being about what will happen at the end of time (Daniel 7–12; Revelation; 1 Enoch). Apocalyptic thought is common in the New Testament (e.g., Matthew 24; Mark 13; 1 Thessalonians 4; Revelation).

Apocrypha (pl. noun; sg. **Apocryphon**; adj. **apocryphal**) – From Greek, *apokryphos* (hidden away; obscure; kept secret). The Apocrypha is a group of Jewish writings included in the Greek translation of the Old Testament, the Septuagint, but not in the Jewish Bible (in Hebrew they are therefore called *sefarim hisoniyyim* [the outside books]). Among them are history books (Maccabees), wisdom books (Ben Sira and Wisdom of Solomon), and tales (Tobit, Judith). They are also called "deuterocanonical" (Greek, "second canon"). See chapter 2.

Aramaic – A northwest Semitic language, closely related to Hebrew, that came to be used widely in the ancient Near East during the Persian Period (539–333 BCE) and continued to be used later on. Some small parts of the Old Testament are written in Aramaic. Jesus and his followers spoke Aramaic.

Babylonian exile – In 587 BCE, the Neo-Babylonian king Nebuchadnezzar conquered Jerusalem, destroyed the First Temple built by King Solomon, and brought the elite population into exile. In 539 BCE, Babylon fell to the Persian king Cyrus the Great, and a year later, in 538 BCE, the exiles were allowed to return home (see Ezra 1:1–4; 6:1–5). The Babylonian exile thus lasted from 587 to 538 BCE and divides the history of ancient Israel into the First Temple and Second Temple periods. See chapter 1.

2 Baruch – A Jewish apocalypse from the late first century CE, written in response to the destruction of the Second Temple in 70 CE. So called to distinguish it from 1 Baruch, or simply the book of Baruch, which is part of the Apocrypha. Closely related to 4 Ezra. See chapter 2.

BCE – The abbreviations BCE (Before the Common Era) and CE (Common Era) have now widely replaced BC (Before Christ) and AD (the Latin *anno Domini* [in the year of our LORD]).

Ben Sira – A Jewish book, written around the year 180 BCE, known in Hebrew as the Wisdom of Ben Sira, in Greek as Sirach, and in Latin as Ecclesiasticus. The book was written in Hebrew in Jerusalem by Jesus son of Eleazar son of Sira (Ben Sira 50:27). The Greek translation is part of the Apocrypha. Sections of the Hebrew book were discovered among the Dead Sea Scrolls. It belongs to the Jewish wisdom books. See chapter 5.

Book of the Watchers – An early Jewish apocalypse written around the year 300 BCE and found in 1 Enoch 1–36, the Book of the Watchers tells the story of the fallen angels, or Watchers (so called because they never sleep), who came to earth to mate with human women (Genesis 6:1–4). See chapter 2.

canon (noun; adj. **canonical**) – Greek, *kanon* (measuring rod); a loanword from Hebrew, *qaneh* (reed). An official, closed list of authoritative (or, in theological language, inspired and therefore sacred) books of Scripture. The term canon has subsequently come to be used for any collection of authoritative books, just as the adjective canonical is often synonymous with authoritative.

CE – *See* BCE.

Christ – Greek, *christos* (the anointed). *See* Messiah.

Christian (noun) – Greek, *christianos* (one belonging to Christ). The word is found three times in the New Testament, in Acts 11:26, 26:28, and 1 Peter 4:16, where it is used for the followers of Jesus, those who have come to believe that Jesus is the Messiah of Israel. The term has remained, but in its earliest use in the New Testament it does not imply the existence of Christianity as its own independent religion.

Christology (noun; adj. **christological**) – Greek, *christos* (the anointed) and –*logia* (the teaching of). The Christian theological teaching about the nature of Christ; that part of Christian theology that explores the nature and person of Jesus and the meaning of his life, death, and resurrection.

codex (sg. noun; pl. **codices**) – Latin, *codex* (book; document). An ancient manuscript containing separate handwritten sheets that are bound along one edge, like a modern book. Whereas early Christians used codices, Jews continued to write their texts on scrolls.

Cyrus the Great (personal name) – The Persian king who conquered Babylon in 539 BCE (documented in the famous Cyrus Cylinder), brought an end to the Babylonian exile, and in 538 BCE issued a verdict allowing all exiles to return home and rebuild the temple in Jerusalem (see Ezra 1:1–4; 6:1–5). In Isaiah 45:1, Cyrus is called God's "anointed" (Hebrew, *mashiach*), who acted on God's behalf to secure the return of the exiles. See chapter 1.

Dead Sea Scrolls – A group of ancient Jewish manuscripts discovered in the 1940s and 1950s on the northwestern shore of the Dead Sea. Dating, for the most part, from the second century BCE to the year 68 CE, when the community was destroyed by the Romans, the manuscripts include the writings of an ancient Jewish sect, possibly an offshoot of the Essenes, as well as the oldest biblical manuscripts. See chapter 2.

deuterocanonical – *See* Apocrypha.

diaspora (noun) – Greek, *diaspora* (scattering; dispersion). Whereas the term exile connotes an enforced, mostly temporary banishment from one's country, the term diaspora refers to the permanent home of the Jews away from the land of Israel. In the Old Testament, Esther and Daniel 1–6 are set in the diaspora (see also John 7:35) and may reflect a distinct lifestyle of Jews in the diaspora.

ecclesia (sg. noun; pl. **ecclesiae**) – Greek, *ekklesia* (assembly), from Greek, *ek–* (out) and *kalein* (to call). In the Septuagint, *ekklesia* means "the assembly of Israelites" (Hebrew *qahal*); in the New Testament, *ekklesia* means "the church; the body of Christians" (see Matthew 16:18; 1 Corinthians 11:22).

ecclesiology (noun) – Greek, *ekklesia* (assembly) and *-logia* (the teaching of). The teaching of the nature and organization of the church.

1 Enoch – Also known as the Ethiopic Apocalypse of Enoch, 1 Enoch is a collection of several early Jewish apocalypses, dating from the third century BCE to the first century CE, and attributed to the antediluvian patriarch Enoch (see Genesis 5:21–24). See chapter 2.

eschatology (noun; adj. **eschatological**) – Greek, *eschatos* (farthest; hindmost). Teaching about the last things. Eschatology is concerned with the end of time and the events that, according to Jewish and Christian belief, God has ordained to unfold at the end of history: divine intervention, the restoration of Israel, resurrection, the great judgment, and the angelic afterlife.

Essenes – A Jewish sect in ancient Israel, from the second century BCE to the first century CE. According to Philo and Josephus, the Essenes lived primarily in cities, were highly organized, were obedient to their elders, practiced celibacy, and shared communal property. Many scholars believe that the Dead Sea Scrolls community were Essenes.

evangelist – From Greek, *euangelion* (good news); lit. "the proclaimer of good news," though most commonly used for the authors of the four Gospels in the New Testament.

exegesis (noun; adj. **exegetical**) – Greek, *exegesis* (explanation; interpretation), from Greek *ex–* (out of) and *hegeisthai* (to guide, lead). The critical exposition or interpretation of a (usually biblical) text.

4 Ezra – A Jewish apocalypse from the late first century CE, written in response to the destruction of the Second Temple in 70 CE. Closely related to 2 Baruch. See chapter 2.

First Temple, First Temple period – Built by King Solomon in the tenth century BCE in Jerusalem (1 Kings 8), the First Temple served as the center for Israel's sacrificial worship until it was destroyed by the Babylonian king Nebuchadnezzar in 587 BCE. The First Temple period lasted from the tenth to the sixth century BCE. See chapter 1.

Galilee – The northernmost region of Israel, including the Sea of Galilee, just south of modern-day Syria and Lebanon.

Gospel (noun) – Middle English, *godspell*; translation of Greek, *euangelion* (good tidings). Originally the good news about the life and death of Jesus (Romans 1:1), the term came to mean the written accounts of Jesus. In addition to the four Gospels in the New Testament (Matthew, Mark, Luke, and John), there are several apocryphal Gospels, among them the Gospel of Thomas and the Gospel of Judas.

halakhah – Hebrew, *halakhah* (the way to behave), from Hebrew, *halakh* (to go). Halakah refers to the legal texts in rabbinic Judaism and, more generally, to any legal decision according to Jewish law (Torah).

Hasmoneans – Also known as the Maccabees, the Hasmoneans were a family of priests who in 167–164 BCE launched an uprising, known as the Maccabean revolt, against the Seleucid (Greek) ruler Antiochus IV Epiphanes, who had desecrated the Jerusalem temple. They recaptured the temple (commemorated by the festival of Hanukkah). The Hasmonean dynasty ruled over Judea for about a century, until Jerusalem was taken by the Romans in 63 BCE. Their story is told in the apocryphal books of 1 and 2 Maccabees and by the first-century Jewish historian Josephus.

Hebrew Bible – Whereas Christians speak of the Old Testament, Jews and most scholars today prefer the term Hebrew Bible, which is more descriptive and less denominational. The Hebrew Bible/Old Testament survives in more than one form. The most important text versions are the Masoretic Text (MT) and the Septuagint (LXX). See chapter 2.

Hellenism, Hellenization, Hellenistic period – Greek, *hellen* (Greek); also *hellenismos* (being/becoming Greek). The Hellenistic period, a time of Greek rule and dominance, lasted from 332 BCE, the time of Alexander the Great, to 63 BCE, when the Romans took Jerusalem. The term Hellenism refers broadly to the advancement of the Greek language, culture, lifestyle, and politics. Greek *Hellenismos* is found in the apocryphal book of 2 Maccabees 4:13, where it is used in contrast of Greek *Ioudaismos* (Judaism). See chapter 1.

Jew – *See* Judaism.

Josephus (personal name) – Ca. 37–100 CE, a Jewish Hellenistic historian, prolific author, and principal witness of Judean culture in the Roman period. His *Jewish Antiquities* is a twenty-volume Jewish history spanning the period from creation to the Jewish revolt against Rome. His *Jewish War* is a gripping account of the revolt against Rome (66–70 CE) that failed and resulted in the destruction of Jerusalem and the burning of the temple in 70 CE.

Jubilees – A Jewish book from the second century BCE that retells the biblical stories from the creation account in Genesis 1 to Israel at Mount Sinai in Exodus 20. Several copies were found among the Dead Sea Scrolls. See chapter 2.

Judaism – Greek, *Ioudaismos* (Judaism). The term first occurs in the apocryphal book of 2 Maccabees 2:21, 8:1, and 14:38. See also in the New Testament Galatians 1:13. In antiquity, Greek *Ioudaios* (pl. *Ioudaioi*; Latin *Iudaeus*, pl. *Iudaei*; from Hebrew *Yehudi*) was primarily an ethnic/geographic term for the inhabitants of *Ioudaia* (Judea). Since the Second Temple period the term has been used for those who are not ethnically or geographically from Judea.

Judea or **Judah** (adj. **Judean**; sometimes spelled **Judaean**) – Hebrew, *Yehuda*. A region in southern Israel, south of Samaria. After the death of King Solomon in 922 BCE, the united monarchy built by King David broke into two, the northern kingdom of Israel and the southern kingdom of Judea, with Jerusalem as its capital.

law – English translation of Greek *nomos*. *See* Torah.

LXX – *See* Septuagint.

Maccabees – *See* Hasmoneans.

Masoretic Text – Abbreviated MT, the Masoretic Text is the scholarly designation of the Hebrew text of the Old Testament. So named after the Masoretes, Jewish scribes who from the seventh to the eleventh century CE copied and preserved the biblical text. The MT is often compared to the Septuagint (LXX), another important witness to the text of the Old Testament.

messiah (noun; adj. **messianic**) – Hebrew, *mashiach* (anointed); Greek, *christos* (the anointed), from which comes the English word "Christ." In the Old Testament, kings, priests, and some prophets were anointed into office. During the Second Temple period, the term came to designate a savior figure of the end time. See chapter 3.

messianism – Hebrew, *mashiach* (anointed). The Jewish belief in a divine agent whom God will send at the end of time to reign over a restored kingdom of Israel. *See also* Christology. See chapter 3.

Midrash (noun) – From Hebrew, *darash* (seek; study). Designates both the art of Jewish interpretation of a biblical text that goes beyond the plain meaning of the text and the interpretive text itself that results from it.

Mishnah (noun) – From Hebrew, *shanah* (repeat), hence "study by repetition." The Mishnah is the first major rabbinic document, edited ca. 200 CE, a compilation of oral traditions that are organized thematically and that go back to the time of the Second Temple in Jerusalem. The Mishnah is the basis for the Jerusalem Talmud and the Babylonian Talmud.

Old Testament – *See* Hebrew Bible.

passion narrative – From Latin, *passio* (suffer; endure). The final accounts in the four Gospels of Jesus's entry into Jerusalem and his arrest, trial, crucifixion, and burial. See Matthew 26–27, Mark 14–15, Luke 22–23, and John 18–19.

Passover – *See* Pesach.

Pentateuch (noun) – Greek, *pentateuchos* (five scrolls). The scholarly designation for the first five books of the Bible: Genesis, Exodus, Leviticus, Numbers, and Deuteronomy. *See* Torah.

Persian period – A period of Persian rule over the ancient Near East during the Second Temple time, from 539 BCE, when Cyrus the Great defeated Babylon, to 333 BCE, when the Persians were defeated by the Greek king Alexander the Great. See chapter 1.

Pesach – Hebrew, *pasach* (pass over), hence English *Passover*. The biblical festival commemorating the exodus from Egypt (Exodus 12). In the New Testament, Jesus is identified as the paschal lamb (1 Corinthians 5:7), the lamb sacrificed at

Passover, the time during which Jesus was crucified (Mark 14:12).

Pharisees – Hebrew, *parash* (separate). One of three Jewish movements during the Second Temple period mentioned by Josephus (besides the Sadducees and the Essenes), the Pharisees were concerned with the rigorous and accurate interpretation of Jewish law. After the destruction of the Second Temple in 70 CE, Pharisaic teachings became foundational for the formation of rabbinic Judaism. Portraits of the Pharisees in the New Testament tend to be hostile. The apostle Paul says that he was a Pharisee (Philippians 3:5; see also Acts 23:6; 26:5).

Philo of Alexandria (personal name) – Ca. 20 BCE–50 CE, a Jewish Hellenistic philosopher from Alexandria, Egypt, prolific author, and prominent member of the large Alexandrian Jewish community. He is best known for his allegorical interpretations of the Jewish Bible, through which he attempted to integrate his ancestral tradition with Hellenistic philosophy.

Pseudepigrapha (pl. noun; sg. **Pseudepigraphon**; adj. **pseudepigraphic**) – Greek, *pseudepigraphos* (having a false title; falsely attributed writing). A designation commonly used by scholars for diverse ancient Jewish and Christian books that are not part of the Old Testament, the Septuagint, or the New Testament. Most of these texts are attributed to ancient figures of the biblical past, even though they were actually written at a much later time, hence the designation "falsely attributed writing." See chapter 2.

Qumran – Never mentioned in the Bible, Qumran is the modern, Arabic name for an ancient site located on the northwestern shore of the Dead Sea. The site was home to the Jewish sect, possibly an offshoot of the Essenes, that left us the Dead Sea Scrolls. See chapter 2.

rabbi – Aramaic, *rabbi* (my great one; my teacher). A title used by a student to address a Jewish teacher. In New Testament times, rabbis were Jewish teachers of the Torah and its commentaries. In the Gospels, the disciples call Jesus rabbi (e.g., Matthew 26:25, 49; Mark 9:5; John 1:38).

rabbinic Judaism – Following the destruction of the Jerusalem temple in 70 CE, the rabbis organized a form of Judaism without a temple that focused on daily prayer, Torah study, and services in the synagogue. Over the centuries, the rabbis produced several texts that remain foundational to this day, among them the Mishnah and the Talmud.

revelation (noun) – From Latin, *revelare* (reveal; disclose); Greek, *apokalypsis* (uncovering), hence the English word apocalypse. The disclosure of something previously unknown to a human being by God or an angel. Revelation is also (capitalized) the title of the last book of the Christian Bible.

Roman period – The final part of the Second Temple period, beginning in 63 BCE with the Roman rule over Judea.

Sabbath – *See* Shabbat.

Sadducees – Sometimes derived from Hebrew *zaddiq* (righteous), though more commonly derived from the name Zadok, the priest of David (2 Samuel 20:25; 1 Kings 4:4). A Jewish movement that existed from the second century BCE to the destruction of the Jerusalem temple in 70 CE, active around the temple in Jerusalem. Josephus claims that the Sadducees came from upper social and economic Judean society. Unlike the Pharisees, the Sadducees rejected the interpretation of the Torah and the belief in the resurrection (Mark 12:18). See chapter 6.

Samaria, Samaritans – The descendants of the population of Samaria in northern Israel, after the Assyrians invaded the region and deported its inhabitants in 722 BCE. The Samaritans consider themselves descendants of the Jewish remnant, whereas those who returned from the Babylonian exile regarded them as descendants of foreigners. The Samaritans worship on Mount Gerizim. Their Bible consists only of the Torah. A fairly small Samaritan population still lives in Israel today.

Satan – Hebrew, *satan* (adversary; accuser). In the Old Testament, a heavenly figure subordinate to God who tests humans (Job 1). By the time of the New Testament, Satan has become a supernatural being opposed to God (Mark 3:19–27).

Scripture – Latin, *scriptura* (a writing). A biblical passage or a book that is considered inspired and authoritative. Since the biblical canon was put together long after the books of the Bible were written, it is anachronistic to speak of a Bible during biblical times. Most scholars of early Judaism therefore prefer to speak of Scriptures instead of the Bible when they refer to the authoritative books that later became biblical.

scroll – In early Judaism, texts were written on scrolls, not in codices or books. A scroll is a long strip of parchment (parchment is the treated skin of an animal) sewn together from smaller pieces and rolled up. The text is written in columns directly onto the parchment. The scroll is read by unrolling one side while rolling up the other. To this day, Torah scrolls are used in synagogues around the world.

Second Temple, Second Temple period – The Second Temple in Jerusalem, built after the exiles returned from the Babylonian exile, was inaugurated in 515 BCE. The Second Temple was destroyed by the Romans in 70 CE. The Second Temple period thus lasted from the sixth century BCE to the first century CE. See chapter 1.

Septuagint – From Latin, *septuaginta* (seventy), hence the use of the Roman numeral LXX as an abbreviation. The earliest Greek translation of the Jewish Scriptures. Tradition holds that the translation of the Torah was done by seventy-two elders. The translation began in the third century BCE. The LXX includes some books not contained in the Hebrew Old Testament (or Masoretic Text), which are known as the Apocrypha. The LXX became the Bible of the early Christians and remains the Old Testament of several churches, including the Roman Catholic Church. See chapter 2.

Shabbat (noun) – Hebrew, *shabbat* (cease; rest). The Sabbath day (see Exodus 20:8–11; 35:1–3).

Shema (noun) – Hebrew, *shema* (Hear!). Name of a prayer in Judaism that the faithful are instructed to recite twice daily, named after its first line (Deuteronomy 6:4), "Hear, O Israel: The LORD is our God, the LORD is one." The prayer is composed of Deuteronomy 6:4–9, 11:13–21, and Numbers 15:37–41. In the Gospels, the commandment to love God (Deuteronomy 6:5) and neighbor (Leviticus 19:18) epitomizes the Mosaic Torah (Matthew 22:34–40; Mark 12:28–34). See chapter 5.

Sirach – See Ben Sira.

Son of Man – From Hebrew, *ben adam* (mortal). Whereas in the Old Testament (Psalm 8 and in the prophet Ezekiel) "son of man" refers to a human being, in Daniel 7:13–14 the Aramaic phrase *bar enosh* refers to a heavenly being "like a human being." By the time of the New Testament, the term had become a messianic title (Matthew 8:20; 18:11; Mark 2:10; Luke 9:26; John 1:51; 5:27).

supersessionism – Also known as "replacement theology," supersessionism is the Christian belief that the Christian church has superseded, or replaced, the Jewish people; the church has become the new Israel. A common prooftext in the New Testament is Galatians 6:14–16. See chapter 7.

synagogue (noun) – Greek, *synagoge* (a bringing together; assembly), from Greek *sun-* (together) and *agein* (bring). A consecrated building where the community meets to assemble for prayer, Torah reading, study, and learning. According to Luke

4:16, Jesus routinely went to the synagogue on the Sabbath day. See chapter 3.

Synoptic Gospels – Greek, *synopsis* (seeing all together), from Greek *sun–* (together) and *opsis* (seeing). The Gospels of Matthew, Mark, and Luke are known as the Synoptic Gospels, or simply the Synoptics, because they tell many of the same stories about Jesus, often in the same order and in similar language. The Gospel of John typically differs. The attempt to explain the exact literary relationship between the three Synoptic Gospels is called the "synoptic problem."

Talmud – From Hebrew, *lamad* (study; learning). The title of two foundational texts of rabbinic Judaism that originated in two centers of rabbinic study, the lands of Israel and Babylonia: the Jerusalem Talmud, also known as the Palestinian Talmud (compiled ca. 400 CE in Galilee), and the Babylonian Talmud, or Bavli (completed after 500 CE). The work of compiling the Talmuds began in 200 CE. They include comments on, and extensions to, the Mishnah, as well as materials on many other topics.

Temple – The centralized place of sacrificial worship in Jerusalem. The First Temple was built by King Solomon and destroyed by Nebuchadnezzar (922–587 BCE), and the Second Temple was built after the return of the exiles from Babylon and destroyed by the Romans (515 BCE–70 CE).

Tetragrammaton – Greek *tetragrammaton* ([consisting of] four letters). A scholarly designation for the name of the God of Israel in the Old Testament. The Hebrew is typically transliterated as YHWH and rendered in most English translations "the LORD" (in small caps). Observant Jews do not pronounce the Tetragrammaton. The etymology of the Hebrew word is unknown; possibly of the verb "to be; to exist; to come to pass."

Torah – Hebrew, *torah* (instruction; teaching). A term referring broadly to Jewish instruction (Proverbs 1:8) or legal rulings

(Deuteronomy 17:11). More commonly, the term Torah designates the first division of the Jewish Bible, also known as the Pentateuch, comprising the books Genesis, Exodus, Leviticus, Numbers, and Deuteronomy. Apart from a few words, the Torah is written entirely in Hebrew. In the Septuagint, *torah* is commonly translated as *nomos* (law). See chapter 5.

YHWH – *See* Tetragrammaton.

Index of Authors and Subjects

Index of Ancient Names and Places

Zechariah, the priest, 80
Zedekiah, King, 18

Zeus Olympius, 23
Zion, 61

Index of Ancient Text

CPSIA information can be obtained
at www.ICGtesting.com
Printed in the USA
BVHW040349190619
551366BV00015B/188/P